# Tarot Life Saver

An Intuitive Journey of Self Discovery

by

Susanna Dark

Susanna Dark

## CONTENTS

*Introduction*

| | |
|---|---|
| 1. My Story | 6 |
| 2. My Introduction to The Tarot | 14 |
| 3. Intuitive Tarot Reading | 33 |
| 4. Time for Change | 44 |
| 5. What is Illness? | 51 |
| 6. Why do We Want to Heal Others | 80 |
| 7. Moving On and a Time for Expansion | 96 |

*Afterword*
*Appendix*

# ACKNOWLEGEMENT

### With Thanks and Love

This book would not have been made possible without all the people that have come into my life since I have been working as an intuitive Tarot reader. All the clients that I have read for in any capacity.
You have all been an inspiration to me.
I have also met many wonderful people whilst running my shop "Wise Old Crow". Customers who give me such lovely feedback on the products that we sell, and those that trust me with the advice and guidance as they start on their spiritual pathway.
I would like to thank the following people. You have blessed my life.
Lyndsey at Yin Yang for letting me read from her beautiful shop.
My spiritual mothers Lin and Barbara for kicking me up the backside when I needed pushing forwards in my work.
Wendy and Karen, without you both, this book would not have been written.
To the ladies in my Tarot group. You have been a pleasure to work with. You have allowed me humility but also helped me become more confident in my abilities.

Lastly to the most important people, my parents. I love you.


Love and Blessings. Sue x

# INTRODUCTION

In this book I want to share with you something new, a healing revelation. A Tarot life saver.

I want to show you how working with a pack of Tarot cards could help change you. I want to explain to you how it can transform your way of thinking and how forming a relationship with the Tarot can heal you. It can heal your emotional suffering, release physical pain, and bring forth revelations. This can be achieved simply by changing your thought processes. The effect and the results can be dramatic.

When people think of the Tarot it generally conjures up an image of divination and fortune telling. We would all like to be able to do readings for ourselves and others. The aim of this book is to share with you a process that is easy to do and which will help you connect to the cards, and that by using this process you will experience accuracy and insight into your readings by forming your own personal meanings to the Tarot cards.

By connecting to a place within you all the answers to your questions can be found, to everything. This place is also where illness stems from but it is also the place from where healing comes.

Looking at an image on a Tarot card for ten minutes at a time and focusing on one Tarot card a week has the possibility to

Susanna Dark

bring major changes to the way you see yourself, your life and others.

In this book we shall be looking at illness, its possible causes, give examples of illnesses, and then look at how to start perceiving illness differently. We will be looking at becoming more aware of where illness comes from, so you can start to control it, rather than it controlling you.

I know it sounds amazing, scary and crazy. It is a dramatic claim, but trust me and read on, for I have taught this process to others and I have seen the results.

To know ourselves makes us better equipped to know others and to understand more clearly the lives we live. This understanding then helps us to be able to make better life choices for ourselves which can then impact positively on those around us.

I shall be sharing my personal experiences with you and how working with the Tarot has helped me through some challenging times in my life. I shall also be sharing examples of how it has helped others that I have come into contact with during my time as a professional Tarot reader.

The tarot deck that I shall be working with throughout this book is "The Tarot of the Old Path", but, due to copywrite, I am unable to feature pictures of this deck.

Throughout this book I shall be using the word Magick, spelt with a K. This is to differentiate from the more usual form of the word "magic", the more familiar practice used in conjuring acts by great magicians such as the late Paul Daniels.

The Magick I wish to refer to is the Magick that we all have within, the Magick of intuition, intent and inner power.

Susanna Dark

# CHAPTER 1

## My Story

I was born on a snowy winter's day, back in February 1966. I very nearly didn't make it into the world. I was nearly strangled in the womb due to the umbilical cord being wrapped around my throat. Even at that time I had a stubbornness. I wanted to lay in my mother's womb my way, the way I felt comfortable. Even then I wanted things differently to the norm!
I felt I had the deciding factor as to how I would be born which was bottom first, but it was my mother who at the time had the ultimate decision whether to push or not. Something inside her, whether you would describe it as an unspoken message or an instinctive thought, told her not to push. The nurse at the hospital discovered my potential Hanged Man predicament and this was then quickly rectified with a dis-entanglement and the use of forceps, much to my mother's great discomfort. When I did eventually come into this world, I did not enter as a being of what would be considered physical perfection.
I had six fingers on each hand and six toes on one foot. My mother reminded me of this when I was young and told me how I was quickly rushed off into a separate room where I had my extra fingers snipped off, and how I screamed the whole place down when they were removed. (They were flaps of skin with little stubby bones at the end which they did not remove.) Not only did I have extra fingers, but I had an extra toe on my right foot too. The extra toe situation had been operated on once, but it appeared to be impossible to remove as it kept

growing back! The bone did not want to die. Not only did the operating staff have the extra toe to rectify, but I also had been born with a gap in my spine and a club foot. (The club foot was eventually rectified in childhood surgery).

I was told that nothing could be done for the slight gap in my spine, but that in later years I may have to wear a built-up shoe, to aid my walking.

As I grew up into my early years, it was also discovered that I had a shadow on my lung. This was to be treated by medication and regular chest X-rays, and I remember at the time, as a child standing in front of a prehistoric, huge, freezing cold X-Ray machine, feeling so very fearful and not understanding what was going on. Was this X-Ray machine a robot that was going to crush me? It sure sounded like a robot with its inane, rumbling noise. The shadow on the lung then lead at the age of eight to asthma, and then the asthma lead to eczema.

However, even with all these impairments I was a happy child. I had a very optimistic disposition. Nothing used to get me down. My mother often commented how amazed she was that I was this way inclined. I had, in my mother's eyes, so many things wrong with me, how could I function in this world?

My cup was always half full so to speak. It was as though I was aware, even from my early years, of life's simplicities. That life was merely illusion and not worth getting stressed over.

I was exposed to and very much aware of my illnesses and physical impairments from a very early age. I was aware that I was not the same as other children. I found it difficult to interact with them and at school I did not have many friends. At one point, at the age of eleven I could honestly say I had none.

So ashamed was I of my disfigured foot that I would dread swimming lessons. I would stand with the other children, bare footed at the edge of the pool, with one foot standing over the other trying to hide the disfigured foot. My teacher would then tell me to "Stand Up straight!" and I would die with embarrassment, not understanding at that age that no one

Susanna Dark

would be interested in looking at my foot. It was just part of me, and not the whole me. But at that young age image is so very important. All children want to look perfect and fit in with the others and to feel the same. I was not the same and I knew it.

I would dread break times at school where we had to go outside in the playground because I would have no one to talk to. I would roam the grey, concrete playground, head down, watching other children play in their groups but feel unable to interact and to share in their world. What were they playing, saying and thinking? I had no part of it. I did not understand it nor did I fit into it.

I was an outsider and as such I got bullied at school by some of the other children. At the age of twelve I began to suffer from hormonal migraines. This often meant that I would leave the class and sit or lay outside until the migraine subsided. When class finished the other children would approach me while I was in a state of slumber and try to wake me or talk to me. I would try to ignore them, which would result in these children spitting on me to gain my attention.

I wonder if the force of destiny, using some sort of invisible hand, fashioned my life so that I was forced to be separate from other children, so that I would not interact with the norm. I would be the eternal spectator. I would understand the different and become part of it. I wonder if by being the spectator I was more able to be tuned in to the unspoken word in some way. I watched others, not listening to their voices, but reading them through their actions.

I know that to you reader this must seem harsh, almost as a mark of judgement, but when we think of our lives and our destiny, I feel that we must see that it has been created with love. Otherwise it would be a very bitter life we live. At the time I definitely did not see my childhood this way.

Yes, at times I was sad and lonely, but I adjusted and found happiness in playing on my own, in my own world of make believe. Sometimes this world of make believe consisted of invisible friends from other worlds, or I would seek out the equally quiet, social rejects in my school year, and we would

Susanna Dark

talk about holding seances in the school toilets, connecting with the dead.
Yes, my life was strange. I was strange as a child. I did not fit in. I belonged somewhere else, but I did not know where.

They say that to be born other-worldy with an interest in the bizarre, you must be born from equally strange parents. I suppose you could say that was true. My mother was a very highly-strung woman and blamed all her failings in life on my father. My father suffered from depression and was equally sensitive. From a root perspective my parents were very much alike, not that my mother would have ever agreed. My father was the enemy and in her view he had ruined her life.

My mother had experienced an unhappy childhood, being the child of a violent father and an unloving mother. She was incredibly naturally intuitive, seeing many things in her childhood from premonitions of fellow school children having road accidents for example to supernatural encounters of spirits lurking under her bed. She would describe hearing old fashioned horse and carts trotting outside her bedroom window on the streets below.
Such was my mother's sensitivity that it upset her greatly, having all these supernatural experiences but not anyone to talk to about it. "It is all in your imagination," was the response from her parents, and "Just go back to sleep", would be another.
When my mother was a child she prayed that the supernatural visions would be taken away, and as such they were.
I remember her telling me how lonely she felt with her parents not understanding her sensitivity, and that was why she decided that if she had children she would be a different kind of mother and would listen to her children and be open to them.
My mother hated her own parents. Her father would often beat her with a belt if she misbehaved. She was not the only one though who her father would take out his frustrations on. My grandmother was also a victim, as was the pet dog. I

remember seeing my grandmother once with a large wound on her eye, where my grandfather had hit her so hard that the glasses she wore imbedded in her eye, nearly causing her blindness. My grandfather suffered from a common illness in the 1940s, that of post war aggression.

My mother had been born in 1939, and as such had seen nothing of her father whilst he was away at war. When he returned home after the war had ended he was a stranger in my mother's eyes. Suddenly to have to obey this stranger, and to see him instantly as her father was something that my mother was obviously unable to do. My mother being the sensitive soul that she was needed to have understanding, love, empathy and most of all, time. But this was not something her father could provide. My mother had a very unhappy childhood.

My father was equally sensitive, but not in the same way that my mother was. My father's sensitivity showed itself in the way of self-judgment, insecurity, and depression.
My father was born in 1940, the result of his mother's affair with a married man and he lived in a surreal home life consisting of a promiscuous mother and a homosexual uncle. In the 1940's/50's this was something that was heavily frowned upon.
In that period of time it was a criminal offence to share your life with someone of the same sex, to be able to be yourself and to love naturally. As a result, in those days gay relationships were hidden in secrecy and shame. As such, growing up in this environment and being a sensitive child, my father wanted everything to be perfect. Bullied at school for being an illegitimate child he craved a life of perfection and normality. If only his life could be normal with a normal mother and father, the same as other children; a normal home life, like other children. My father's home life was far from normal.
When my father was a child, he loved to read the daily newspaper. When it was delivered every morning through the letter box he would eagerly run and grab it from the letter box

and read it with great relish. He would suck in every page, seeking out information on the world, politics and finances. Instead of encouraging his eager curiosity of the world, my grandmother would chastise him, because his uncle wanted the pages to be pristine for reading. My father's uncle wanted to be the first to read the perfect, uncreased, freshly scented paper. And so my father would be made to iron each and every page, to bring the newspaper back to its original perfection.

This was a situation that could have been seen as mental punishment, and an example of an environment where everything had to be perfect. My father grew up in this environment, and as such sought for perfection within himself and others and has continued to do this all his life. He would never find it of course and would punish himself and others on this journey to seek it out.

Both my parents were troubled souls. They had, like most people, not known to look within themselves, to try to find out the source of their unhappiness. In their day, you survived. You just got on with it.

I suppose that from an early age I wanted to make my parents well. I wanted to make them happy and to make them love themselves and each other. But I couldn't, and due to my father's issues from childhood I didn't receive any love from him. He was unable to open up and show affection. I wished that I had owned a magic wand to change my father, to be able to receive some love from him. If I wanted a cuddle I would approach him but this would be reciprocated by a pat on the back. Rigid and closed. Like my father.

Maybe if I had owned a magic wand, I could have magicked it all away. I could have magicked love from my father and magicked my mother and father finding happiness with each other and from life.

I learnt at an early age that you can try and help others, but if they do not want to be helped, then there is nothing you can do.

When I was nine years old, my father beat up my mother. Due to my father's sensitivities and his inability to show his emotions, he used to bottle up all his anger and frustrations with life.

I remember one Saturday in particular. My father had gone to see a football match with my older brother and had arrived home, later than usual from this match. My mother, of equally sensitive disposition had been worried, and thought that they had been in an accident. As soon as they both came in through the front door my mother started to share her worries with my father. The initial worry soon turned into an argument, and my father, unable to express himself vocally, expressed himself violently towards my mother. He beat her around the face until she was black and blue with bruises. At the time my mother was eight months pregnant with my younger brother James. During the beating she had protected her stomach with her hands, and as such laid her face bare and vulnerable. I remember as a child crying watching the beating unfold. My older brother, who was ten years old at the time, jumped on my father's back to try and make him stop attacking my mother, but he was thrown off in the process. I was crying hysterically, "Leave my mummy alone! Leave her alone!". My mother shouted at us to go into the room next door, but of course we were unable to do this.

This was a very unhappy time for the whole family. My father did not control his temper, his temper controlled him. He would go into a rage where all would go black, and he would hardly remember a thing after the violent episode had subsided. Luckily these attacks were few and far between.

Back in 1974 things were very different. If you had an emotional issue you took on that British "stiff upper lip" attitude and carried on regardless.

Susanna Dark

Not many people looked within, to discover themselves. If you did and you spoke about it, then you were thought of as strange, and if you did go for help and to see a psychiatrist, then you were considered mad. No one ever talked about their problems. If you did have an issue you could chat to your doctor, but the doctor may then decide to put you on medication, such as sleeping tablets or anti-depressants. That seemed to be the cure for everything - medication.

When I was eight years old I was experiencing terrible nightmares and I was unable to sleep, so my mother took me to the doctors who prescribed me the drug Phenergan. This was a little blue sleeping tablet that seemed to take away all my fears, but did it really cure me, or did it suppress the fear? An eight-year-old child on sleeping tablets. This is how things were done in the 1970's. A time of knuckling down, rolling up the sleeves and getting on with it, and no complaining. Medication was the cure when in fact it was just a mask.

So there you have it. My early experiences of both physical and mental illness that have fuelled my yearning to heal others.

# CHAPTER 2

## My Introduction to The Tarot

Tarot cards. These days you can find them everywhere. In pound shops, book stores, new age shops.... Even some supermarkets stock them.

We would all like to be able to read them or failing that, seek out a clairvoyant to tell us what they mean. We all want to know what our future holds. We all want love, happiness, hope, money and success and.....breathe..... We want it all don't we?
But what is the point of the Tarot cards? Do they work, or are they a load of rubbish? Are they part of the fortune telling game, a fraudulent system of false hope, preying on the vulnerable? Or are the Tarot cards merely just a game, as they were originally designed to be?

I remember when I held my first deck of Tarot cards back in 1995. Little did I know then how a strange pack of 78 cards would change my life and the lives of others.

At around this time I was spending a day with my friend Carole. Carole was both a friend and a colleague at work while I was working in what I call my "normal" job. It was an office job. This was a job I thought I should do. It was reliable, steadfast and had a guaranteed income. But as I would later find out, it was not for me.

Anyway, back to Carole. She had, in her possession a set of Tarot cards. She had looked at them, but not really done anything with them and after a while had just put them away in a drawer. When Carole was given these cards as a gift, (there is a superstition you are only supposed to be gifted a Tarot deck, not buy them for yourself. Today we know this is not true), she opened the pack with trepidation.

"Wow a set of Tarot cards!", she thought, "Now I have the power!"
She wasn't sure what the power was, but in her mind she had it anyway!

Carole looked at the cards, all 78 of them. There were so many of them, she felt overwhelmed. She then looked at the booklet that came with the set of cards. The booklet contained a brief meaning to each card. But did this booklet contain the meaning to all decks of cards, or just this particular deck she wondered? As she started to read the booklet, Carole realised that it was the guide to this deck only, and the more of the booklet she read, the more bored she was becoming. Her eyes started to gloss over and she became sleepy.
Surely she should be energised by this powerful tool of the occult, but no. Carole was starting to become under stimulated by the words in the booklet. It talked in a straight forward way and included a useful list of all the cards and a concise meaning. It was nothing more and nothing less than a practical guide and was not helping Carole to get the most out of her deck.

Now came the battle with what to do next. She put the cards back in the box, took them back out again, took them out of the box, and back again. This process went on for a while, not leading to anything progressive. The result of the battle was the Tarot deck being put away in a set of drawers, and never coming out again. You know, the set of drawers we have,

where things are put away for a future time. The future that usually ends up with a visit to the charity shop.
This beautiful set of cards, with such powerful stunning imagery which had amazed Carole at the start, but due to the booklet, had left her feeling deflated, confused, and underwhelmed.

Carole knew instinctively that she had something powerful in her hands, something that was supposedly used to entertain and thrill herself and others. But she no idea how to use them, and that little booklet was not giving her any clues.

Back in 1995, the Tarot was still considered a tool of the Occult, and still is by many, even nowadays in our more supposedly open society. It's a spooky thing of fascination, found in such films as the James Bond film, "Live and Let Die". For instance, The Death card was seen by many as a premonition of their own death, and the Lovers card, the card of sex and intimacy. As such the cards were scary things, to be avoided and to fear. And NOT to be messed around with.

If you owned a set of Tarot cards it meant that you were either:
a) A Witch
b) Related to a Witch
c) A Fortune Teller
d) A Crazy Person.

At the time I had a fascination with anything unusual, so when Carole showed me her pack of Tarot cards during a conversation on the subject I felt a strange combination of being petrified, amazed and excited all at once. It was a deck entitled "The Tarot of the Old Path".
Would I be able to see, please? Could I handle it? What would happen to me if I touched it? Would I be harmed in some way? Would it bring me bad luck? All these crazy questions went through my mind. Never before had I been exposed to the power of the occult.

Susanna Dark

Such was the power of the Tarot and the reputation it held. I had never even seen a set of Tarot cards before and back in 1995, that was the norm.

Carole mentioned that it was fine to hold the cards, but that some people can be a little sensitive over other people holding their cards. I wondered why. But, not only did Carole let me hold her Tarot deck, she actually then gifted the deck to me. I NOW had a tarot deck, I NOW had the power of the occult in MY hands. What would I do with this now, and now that I had touched the cards, was there any going back to the world of normality?

I decided that what would be the safest thing to do was to just hold the Tarot cards in my hand and see how they felt. Once the cards were in my hands and I realised that in fact, it was just a set of normal cards, with pretty pictures, I closed my eyes, and tried to get a sense of the cards. To me they felt normal, just like a set of playing cards. Viewing them again, I slowly went through each card, taking in its bizarre but beautiful imagery. No, they were not just a set of pretty pictures, they had hidden messages in them, but at that time I had no idea what the cards meant, if they meant anything at all.

To me at that time, these Tarot cards were a source of fascination. A journey into the unknown. A magical tool of the occult.

Each card showed an image, and each image related to the Major Arcana, or the Minor Arcana. What the heck did that mean? I was confused already!
Apparently, Carole told me, the Major Arcana consisted of such cards as The High Priestess, and The Devil. The Devil card!!! Oh my gosh, now I really was working with a tool of the occult!
The Major Arcana, as its name suggests is all about the major stuff of life. For example, another of the cards is called

Strength, and represents our own inner strength in life. As such the Major Arcana talks of the major qualities and challenges we can encounter through life. Carole started talking more on the Major Arcana, and seeing how distressed I had looked over the Devil card, then read from the little booklet that came with the cards. It explained that the Devil card was in fact all about the negativity that we may encounter in life, the stuff that can enchain us and that stops us from being able to move forwards. Relief! Nothing was going to possess my soul!

The Minor Arcana, separated into the suits of pentacles, cups, swords and wands referred to the minor points in life, that is, money, love, thoughts and work. Combining both the Major Arcana and the Minor Arcana the Tarot spoke of the journey of life.

I started looking at the Major Arcana first, and as I looked at each card I was struck by how beautiful the artwork was. Around the edge of each card were symbols that I did not understand, but I tried to put that to the back of my mind and not be intimidated by them. Best just to bathe in the imagery and power of this beautiful Tarot deck that I was holding. Each card was printed on glossy paper and each card told a story.

I now wanted to find out more about these cards and to study them and learn the meanings of each one. I decided to look at the small paper booklet that came with the Tarot deck. This was obviously the key. But, as I removed the booklet from the box I found that it was thin and lacked the same feeling as the cards. The vibrant colour of each card was missing. The booklet was printed in black and white and was created out of flimsy paper. It had the title of the card, and a meaning next to it but the meaning lacked depth.
I felt it lacked any real connection to the cards at all.
It was like an afterthought in my mind. There was no feeling of power, nothing as powerful as the imagery on the Tarot cards themselves.

Susanna Dark

What would happen if I was to throw this booklet away? No, that was way too scary! Then I really would be in a boat, without a paddle, cast out to sea. The idea was way too frightening. I felt that the booklet and the cards MUST belong together, as part of a package. That it was the intention they must be used this way. Surely?

What would help me, I decided, was to take each Tarot card, and at the bottom of the card, in pencil, copy pointer words from the booklet, showing the meaning. That was the key. Then each Tarot card would be easy to understand and to read. All I would need to do was to work with the Tarot deck itself, pull a card, and there, hey presto, would also be the meaning, ready and waiting for me. After all, the booklet was the Tarot bible for this Tarot deck. The creator of the deck knew the meanings to each card, and the booklet was somewhere that I could refer to and would give me those meanings but would also provide the answer to any problems that I had. The Tarot deck was the key to life!

To read the cards I decided to start by just laying out three cards as a spread in front of me on my table. One card would represent the past, the middle card the present, and the final card the future.

I drew the following cards and then read from the booklet.

*The Hanged Man – Seeing things from a different perspective, alternative viewpoint, self-sacrifice.*

*The Fool – A new beginning, fresh journey, a brave adventure.*

*Strength – Bravery in adversity, inner strength, Self-belief.*

So, every time I read for myself or a friend, on the dealing of each card and by using my notes that I had written in pencil on the bottom of each card, I would be prompted to give the meaning of each card.

Little did I realise how limiting doing this would be. All I had to work with were these trigger statements. Also, little did I

Susanna Dark

realise at the time that by reading the cards in this way with just trigger words on the cards, I was keeping myself small. It was the safe way. It was a beginning, but I did not know it.

After reading for myself a few times, by that I mean successfully finding out the meanings from the Tarot booklet, I decided that I was ready and I would start conducting readings for friends and relatives for practice. This started out ok, but after a while, I was starting to find I was stuck. It would often happen that during a reading a friend would want to know more, or if I read for myself, I would want to know more too. I needed to expand and to get a greater sense of the cards themselves. I realised that my readings had no depth to them. I could not expand on my readings and they were short and had no structure. I was reading parrot fashion.

*"The Fool - A new beginning, fresh journey, a brave adventure."*
End of story!   And likewise with the other cards.

So I decided to put the Major Arcana aside and concentrate now on the Minor Arcana.
I learnt from the booklet all about the suits, and that each suit represented either *Work – Wands, Love – Cups, Swords – Thoughts, or Pentacles – Money.*
But now there was another problem, if I went by the booklet and drew cards that were labelled as associated with work matters BUT then a friend wanted a reading to be about love related issues, how could I possibly give relevant advice?

*For example, I drew the Ace of Wands – "The time to strike now over a new job. A time to change your pathway, career wise."*

Most of my friends were asking me advice on love, and as I was selecting the cards, they all seemed to be Wands cards associated with work life! Perhaps my friend really needed to be told about her working life. I would try that one. Nope, not a good idea! How then could these cards assist me with looking at love? All was starting to really confuse and overwhelm me. I had 78 cards to work with and I felt totally out of my depth. Perhaps the solution was to learn from one of the practical Tarot books on the market. One that tells you the inside out of the Tarot, written by a successful Tarot guru, whose life mission has been to study the Tarot and its every working. I decided to purchase a "One Step Tarot" book but after reading a few pages, I started to find that my brain switched off. The book itself had excellent reviews and I wondered what was wrong with me. Why was I not connecting with it? Surely by studying the Tarot, its imagery, symbology and history this would make me a better reader? I could learn from the masters of the trade. I would have the necessary knowledge to impart in my readings. I would know the exact meanings of the Tarot cards. I could even become a Tarot guru myself!

The more I started to read, the more Tarot books I purchased written by these gurus, the more confused I became. They were just not talking to me. They were talking AT me and my brain was obviously not wired in the analytical way that I thought.
I needed to step off the wheel of repetition. The answer lay not in the books I was purchasing, but in me.
Maybe I was not cracked out to read the Tarot after all. Maybe it was a powerful device for the gifted, or the super intelligent, and I was not one of these. This is when self-judgement started to kick in. I had thoughts on putting my Tarot deck away in that charity shop drawer.
Surely there must be an easier way to learn the Tarot? A way where you can feel your way around the cards yourself. An uncomplicated way. A way that does not confuse or intimidate you where you can be yourself, and explore your way naturally? I mentioned my frustrations and concerns to Carole. Initially she just told me to give them away, and that maybe this was the thing with the Tarot, that only certain folk could use them. After all they had not connected with her. But something she also mentioned made sense. She stopped,

took a deep breath and then looked at me. What she said next connected somewhere within me, even though I was not sure what she meant!

Carole told me that I needed to find a way of connecting to the cards intuitively.

What did she mean? How could I connect to the cards intuitively?

My heart beat began to speed up and I started to feel excited.

I fell upon this at just the right time.

## What is intuition?

*Have you ever had a moment where you felt as though something wasn't right? Perhaps stepping into a car park late at night, or feeling negative around someone without knowing why? And if you've experienced this before, have you shrugged it off, dismissing it as illogical nonsense?*

*As humans, we have learned to believe that rationality is what should prevail when making decisions about anything from crucial business mergers to what to eat for lunch. But what of that "inner voice", that gut feeling, that little something instinctual from within that tells us how we feel beneath those layers of logic?*

*Instinct and Intuition, as I define it, is this:*

- *Instinct is our innate inclination toward a particular behaviour (as opposed to a learned response).*

- *A gut feeling—or a hunch—is a sensation that appears quickly in consciousness (noticeable enough to be acted on if one chooses to) without us being fully aware of the underlying reasons for its occurrence.*

- *Intuition is a process that gives us the ability to know something directly without analytic reasoning, bridging the gap between the conscious and non-conscious parts of our mind, and also between instinct and reason.*

*In essence, we need both instinct and reason to make the best possible decisions for ourselves, our businesses, and our families.*

*Unfortunately, many of us, even when we experience success using this lesser acknowledged part of us, are uncomfortable with the idea of using our instincts as a guidance tool. We are embarrassed to say that we follow hunches, we mistrust the sometimes cryptic messages that our instincts send to us, and consequently we diminish our capacity to leverage the power of our own instincts when we need them most. Our discomfort with the idea of relying on our instincts is based on millennia of cultural prejudice.*

So, to be intuitive, was to work and to act on the above. "To operate from a place of intuition. So when we connect to the Tarot cards, we use the power of intuition, bridging that gap between the conscious and non-conscious parts of our mind, and also between instinct and reason."

Ok I sort of understood it. Again, technical jargon didn't gel with me well.

Now I had found a different but simple way to connect to the cards. In a way this now made sense to me. I had always acted from a gut feeling and sensed my way around people and situations. I had always used my sixth sense to experience techniques, rather than relying purely on a book which is another person's logical explanation. I found it easier to experience and to learn from that.

So now I had a way to learn the Tarot - the intuitive way. But I also had to find a way to do it. How to find a structured step by step process.

One day, during a meeting with another friend, Jo, who was already such an inspiration to me in everyday life, mentioned to me how meditation was working for her. She mentioned that it helped her still her mind, and as such helped her listen to her inner voice, her intuition, and was able to hear and feel the intuitive messages. This process of meditation sounded fascinating in that a process could have such a powerful effect on an individual. I wondered if meditation could work for me. I also wondered if this could be used as part of this intuitive process and help to connect to the Tarot cards. The idea of meditation was alien to me. Wasn't it just for hippies and yoga gurus. What happened it I went to sleep during meditation? Did I have the strength and concentration for it? All logical questions but coming from a place of fear. A fear where I knew that this meditation business could be the key to something important.

I decided to do some research on meditation, and came across some information, and how to conduct it. Also the different types of meditation, and what might work for a beginner.

### What is meditation?

*Meditation is finding a place of peace leading to a sense of quiet within. By listening to relaxing music whilst finding this place of peace, or perhaps following guided instruction, listening to a chant, or musical instrument, or just being completely still and silent, these are all ways to meditate, to find that place of peace and stillness.*

When we are at peace with ourselves then we can be truly relaxed. Our mind is relaxed, and we can then concentrate. Things that would normally stress us out no longer affect us, and we can achieve greater clarity of our lives, who we are, what we want, and how we feel about others in our lives.

Being able to achieve this sense of peace and stillness of the mind for just five minutes a day can really help.

I suggest that the best way to start, when it comes to meditation is with relaxing music. Find a place where you can't be disturbed, dim the lights, lay back on a comfy sofa, or sit upright on a hard- back chair, and put on a piece of your favourite relaxing music. If, initially you go to sleep it does not matter. The fact that you have made that intent to meditate is all that matters. Do not take it from a place of self- judgement. Just be in the moment and enjoy it.

All starts to make more sense, we have become still, the chattering monkeys that usually fill our minds start to leave and we make room for the new. But, if you find that those monkeys are becoming a barrier simply say to yourself.

**" I welcome your attention, but I am in my stillness - let me be"**

I found that something called a guided meditation, where a step by step journey guides you through the meditation worked best for me as a beginner. I found one that really sung to me, especially if I was having a difficult day.

It was called, "Journey to find your happy place." and is included below.

This guided meditation talked to me from a personal level. I found that by reading this meditation my mood improved and made me feel secure and comforted when I was feeling emotionally insecure or vulnerable.

I also found that by recording the meditation on a mobile phone using the voice recorder app was so much easier. I could lie on the sofa and play it back, closing my eyes, and taking it all in.

Before I share this meditation with you, I wanted to tell you about a friend of mine, who has been through many challenging events in her life, from losing her ex-boyfriend to suicide, to helping and aiding her alcoholic mother. To help her cope with this she has a place that she goes to during relaxation called her "Happy Place." This friend has grown in leaps and bounds and found that this happy place was a good place to start on her journey to transformation. A good starting point.

Now back to your "Happy Place". This can be a place in the now or the past where you have felt your strongest, happiest and most at peace.

Perhaps you had a fond relationship with your grandmother, and you can remember being around her house where she cooked fabulous home cooked apple pies. You loved your grandmother, and she loved you and you looked forward to visiting this place every week.

This is a happy place.

Or perhaps you have a favourite tree in the garden. You can climb up to the highest branch and sit amongst the leaves, it is a place of security and seclusion from everything and everyone else.

This is your happy place.

Susanna Dark

This is the Happy Place Meditation, written by my dear friend Tareth, who has been an inspiration to me. We would often talk about illness and healing, and he helped me, at a challenging time in my life.

You can find the meditation in his book "Alchemy and the Grail," where you can access your very own "Happy Place".

### Journey to your "Happy Place."

*There are so many ways this meditation can be approached. This is accessed from a place of memory.*

*Memory is a great gift, I know it can sometimes be a painful thing as well as a joyful thing, but it is a gift and enables us to re-create beauty in our body.*

*The process is very simple.*

- *Make it clear to all that you cannot be disturbed. Find a place eg your bedroom or a quiet space outside, ensure that all mobile phones are turned off or put to silent. Be still and sit quietly in a quiet space.*

- *Start to remember a place where you love to be. It may be a corner of a room in your house or garden, it may be a place you visited many years ago, where you felt wonderful. You can change it and choose a different place each time you visit your happy place. The important thing is to remember being in a place where you felt good.*

- *Recall what it looks like, do not slip into the danger of thinking you have to see pictures. That is not true. Just recall what it looks like. For example, if I asked you to recall what your mobile phone looks like, you can see it in your mind's eye even if you do not have a picture.*

- *Once you have recalled a bit of what it looks like, go to the phase that is the most important, remember what you felt like the last time you used it.*

- *Take some gentle, deep breaths. As you breathe out, release and relax.*

- *Let your body remember what it felt like or feels like in this place, what your emotions are like, (emotions are calmer in a place you like, the noise in the mind calmer) Just remember being in a nice place, and, on some breaths, feel it.*

*(As you do this, you will create brain chemistry that is the opposite of stress. You will release chemicals of calmness into your body. You will calm everything down)*

- *When you have remembered and felt this place, embrace it, think of it as your happy place, your inner sanctuary.*

- *Think of it as a memory which is like a room inside you, a room you can always go to whenever you wish. ( The nice thing about a memory is that you do not need to have anything physical, you can access it any time, wherever you are. So your sanctuary/happy place is a room in your thoughts. It is a room within you).*

- *When you enter it, make mental note in your mind. "This is my happy place. No one enters here without my permission." This is your place, a place where you can have quality time, dedicated to you ONLY.*

Susanna Dark

*As you say it, feel what that does to you. Feel what it says to your cells, your body, your circulation, your mind. It says "this is a safe place, based on a good feeling, and nothing is allowed in here."*

- *When you have made that statement, take a deep breath, release the breath and relax.*

(Once you have owned your sanctuary/happy place, you can take steps to use it. Simple beginnings. Try to remember that the most important thing about it is that it is just a place to be, a place to be in and to be safe, based on real experience. It is naturally self healing, so you can therefore use it in a simple way for self healing.)

- *Think about things that you would like to place into your sanctuary for help. Think about any aspect of your life that you feel you would like healing for. Bring it to your mind, bring it into your room, into your sanctuary and simply ask for healing to come and be given to help you with this. ( Do not complicate this process. Start with the simple act of asking for healing)*

I hope that you like this Happy Place meditation. When I used it, it made me feel calm and safe. I liked the idea of guided meditations and they worked for me.

I now knew that I needed to find a guided meditation to use with the intuitive Tarot system, and if I could combine the two I knew that this intuitive Tarot reading system could work. I then discovered that there were in fact three guided meditations that I needed:-

1. Opening up

2. The actual guided meditation to connect to the cards themselves

3. Closing down and grounding.

The first of these guided meditations and the first part of the intuitive process is called "Opening Up." This needs to be done before any further intuitive work is done.

But when I first read the term "Opening up" I didn't really understand it. What did "opening up" mean? It sounded like the first stages of surgery to me, but after researching, it appeared that it meant to relax and unfold like a butterfly. Yes, it was a form of surgery but of the psyche, not the physical body, and that the reason behind "opening up" was to conduct a process, to be at peace, to open the mind, and as such become more receptive to your meditation and intuition.

I found the exercise below and it seemed to work.

### Opening up

*Ensure that you are sitting comfortably on a hard-backed chair.*

*Have both your feet on the floor, legs uncrossed.*

*Imagine you are a tree, and that the roots of the tree are connecting to your feet, steadying you and strengthening you.*

*Take a deep breath in and relax.*

*Picture in your mind, a ball of light that travels up from your feet, along your legs and to the base of your spine.*

*Now imagine this ball of light now travelling up from your spine to your stomach. As it travels it grows in size, to a powerful magical light.*

*The ball of light now travels from your stomach to your heart.*

*Now the light moves to your throat. Glowing.*

*Then imagine the light moving to what they call the all-seeing eye, located in the middle of your forehead (sounded strange but I went with it)*

*Lastly the light moves to the top of your head and you feel the top of your head opening.*

*Now finally imagine yourself opening up like a newly born butterfly.*

*Now as we are ready to start, smile and open your eyes ready to embrace a brand new day.*

Well this process was fabulous. I felt that by conducting this guided meditation I was instantly relaxed and at peace. I felt balanced within. On its own, the meditation screamed happiness, so to use it in conjunction with the intuitive Tarot card process I felt it would really work. Initially I read the words to myself, then found that this disturbed what I wanted to achieve, so I read the words aloud using the voice recorder app on my phone. Then I just played it every time I needed to "Open Up".

Next comes the main part of the intuitive process, the guided meditation to connect to the cards themselves. I thought long and hard on how this could work. I needed a guided meditation that implemented a process of using the imagination. And then I came upon a fantastic process. (See Chapter Three) It was the answer to all my prayers.

# CHAPTER 3

### Intuitive Tarot Reading

The intuitive way to learning to read the Tarot involves stretching your own intuitive muscles, learning to trust the little nudges your inner voice directs to you, often through your imagination.

To learn your deck you must take each card and travel into it, allowing the deck image to trigger within you stories and journeys, bringing with them messages for your own inner development, as well as for your learning of what the card can mean in a reading.

I believe if you allow your deck talk to you, then the learning you gain in your own life will be invaluable and the practice in trusting your intuition and understanding of your own symbols will transform your ability to read the cards for others, even with cards you haven't yet travelled into.

After a while of doing these specific journeys for yourself, you will find you can look at a card, travel into it and ask for its meaning whilst doing a reading without the need for elaborate visualisations and relaxations, thus gaining a way to hear your own intuitive voice and inner knowing, as it relates to the questions of the person you might be reading for.

I will outline the way to go into a card at first for your own development and the understanding of a card.

Take a notepad and pen and starting a fresh page, head it

### "The Fool. Initial Findings"

Take your deck of cards and remove the first card of the Major Arcana, The Fool. This is a good starting point.

Look at the card closely and make a note of anything that comes to your mind, do not question it but trust. Make a note of the bits that you like and the bits you don't like. Why is this? e.g. Is it the character in the card, their expression, or clothing, or the weather even?

When you have studied the card for a few minutes, write down all your findings.

When you have finished, start a new section or page and write

### "The Fool – Intuitive Journey"

Now you are ready for the next part of the process, where we let our intuition do some of the work during guided meditation. Look at the card again, and then hold it in your hands, close your eyes and relax. You do not need to remember the card in detail so DON'T PANIC! Remember that anything you forget is part of the process. The images that come to you will be the ones you need.

Try to leave your judging mind behind, and just trust that your mind is delivering to you that which you need to see.

Be ready to experience whatever is there, there isn't a right or a wrong image to have, there is only YOUR image.

## The Guided Meditation

*….. get yourself into a comfortable position, close your eyes, make sure that you are seated on a hard-backed chair, and that your feet are placed uncrossed on the floor, feeling the roots of the earth, connecting with your feet.*

*Take a few slow deep breaths, in through your nose, and out through your mouth, and as you breath out, allow yourself to let go of any tension that you may have, in mind or body. All you need to do is relax. Now say to yourself, these words.*

**"From this aspect of creation, from every particle, from every memory, give me a glimpse in this day of my true self. Show me something that helps me understand"**

This is a very powerful and profound statement to make, as by asking to be shown "my true self" you are asking to be taken to a place of inner harmony, where there is no fear and no self-judgement. A place where you can connect with the real you and be shown the answers to the questions that you hold at present; to be shown the meaning of the card you are journeying with.

*Now imagine a brilliant bright light coming from the centre of the earth up into your feet, slowly coming into your body, starting from your feet and moving up to your head. Once you are surrounded with light from the earth, see the same thing happening from above, so that you are surrounded with light from above and below. (This is done as a place of comfort and safety.)*

*Once you are filled with this light from both star and ground, imagine a staircase in front of you going upward. Walk up the stairs and with each step feeling lighter and lighter in weight* you do. At the top see the card in front of you as a doorway, go through the door, go into the card.

Notice now how you feel emotionally in this card, are you happy or sad, confused or elated? How else do you feel? Notice the temperature in the card, the weather, who else is in the card with you. Animals? People? Do you recognise anyone, if not then these are new acquaintances.

Look around and see what images are there. Are there trees in the card? See these images moving, being and doing what they do. As you take in the scene allow it to develop into a vision, a story of the card itself. You can if you wish walk up to any object, person or animal in the card and ask it/them to tell you what the meaning of the card is, and what is the personal message for you.

**This is the important part, you will need to have a meaning of the card, and personal message for you to write in your journal, so do not forget to ask. Perhaps add it to the recording two minutes before the end.**

For the intuitive journey, I would allocate a seven-minute time slot, for working with each card. So, when you record your guided meditation, allocate as such. As mentioned earlier, only look at working with one card per week, as this process is a slow system that needs to unfold organically.

It is through this process that you are discovering your own personal meanings of the cards. You are creating your own book of the Tarot, your life book. You are profoundly connecting to the Tarot in your own personal and unique way.

Now back to the meditation ….

Susanna Dark

*When you have journeyed enough, thank the characters in the card and then see a doorway of light in front of you, as you walk through this doorway, you find yourself at the top of the stairs, of which you walk down, feeling heavier and heavier as you do. When you reach the bottom, see yourself in a bubble of golden light. Feeling your feet on the floor, and back against the backrest, take a deep breath, and then slowly bring your attention back to the room.*

**It is a good idea to record your journey straight away in your journal.**

Record the journey in either drawings or writings, so that you have a record of how the journey went and any messages that were given to you. Once done you can leave it and come back and read it again a few days or weeks later and see if what you received has had any relevance in your life.

You may find that after a visualisation such as this, things come to you whilst relaxing, or when you are about to fall asleep at night, or in your dreams. Make a note in your journal of anything that comes to you in this way. A picture will be building of the scope of what your card can offer you as well as of what you need to be focusing on in your life at the time.

Having worked with this process myself for every card, I started to feel a connection to each of the cards. I was starting to form my own book of Tarot card meanings. I had a brief meaning of the card from when I looked at it initially, and then a deeper meaning from my own meditation.

Each card not only told me the meaning, but there was also a message for me, a personal message about my life and what I needed to know. Each card, each week, brought a message that was so incredibly relevant to me at that particular point of my life. Not only was the message relevant, it was also very powerful from a soul level.

I shall now share with you the results from my own journal. I have selected the most controversial and normally feared card. The Death Card from the Major Arcana

"Initial Findings".

The Grim Reaper stands in the woodland, positioned on an island. Surrounding him is water. On another part of the island is new life, and a new born baby. New life also shows in the form of flowers and fresh vegetation. Flying about the Grim Reaper is a white barn owl, symbolic of spirituality, and intuition. The Grim Reaper waits, to take the soul of the departed, when it is their time.

"Intuitive Journey"

As I journeyed into this card I was surprised to find my surroundings so very different. The Grim Reaper was not in the card, but what I was greeted with, when entering the doorway and the card was a grand family party. All around me were family members that had died. They were exactly as I remembered them from my past. All full of life, vitality and love, they were smiling and were happy. I could also see my cat Storm. This was so incredibly upsetting, but elative at the same time. I literally cried tears of happiness during this meditation.

The greeting that my family gave me was not just an ordinary "Hello" but a full-blown surprise party with balloons and whistles. "Surprise! We have missed you!" they all shouted.

My meaning of this card was that death is illusion and that we do not die. When it is our time we just leave our physical body behind. The soul lives on, and when we die, we meet our loved ones, on the other side. That yes, life can be a party, but that death can be too.

The message I had for me was about change. To change my perspective on that which I feared. To understand that all is not what you believe it to be, and that by looking further and by understanding more about yourself and others that fear is merely illusion.

You may find that when you start journeying with the cards, that initially, you want to work with trigger words or bullet points, and then expand your findings into paragraphs or stories as you become more confident. With practice you will find that your intuition grows and your mind expands.

After conducting this process. You will need to conduct the final part of the meditations, and this is the closing down.

### Closing Down and Grounding

After meditating and working with your tarot, whether it be conducting readings for yourself or others it is important to conduct this Closing Down Meditation.

It tucks you in for the night and makes you feel just right.

*Ensure that you are sitting comfortably on a hard-backed chair*

*Have both your feet on the floor, legs uncrossed.*

*Feel your roots, connecting to the earth beneath you.*

*Take a deep breath in.*

*Now see yourself as the butterfly, slowly and gently close your wings around you.*

*Now see the door to the top of your head, open, now close this firmly.*

*Next look to your third eye, remember it's the eye located at your forehead, now close this door firmly.*

Finally, I had found an intuitive journeying process that worked for me. A process that I could use to discover the powers of the cards, and my own empowerment within. A journey to the cards and into the cards themselves.

I bought myself a lovely brand-new notebook, with a dragon on the front. I decided that if I went into the process with an inner bravery and resilience (represented the power of the dragon) I could achieve what I set out to do which was to connect to the Tarot cards intuitively.

I worked my way gradually through the rest of the Tarot deck, journeying with one Tarot card a week, nothing more. This whole process took me a while, but I wanted to learn each card. This was a personal journey, a pilgrimage of dedication and I wanted to make sure that the Tarot cards were impacting on me from an unconscious level. Also, I would make sure that if I dreamt about a particular card, I would add my findings to my dragon journal. So I kept it by my bed side to use on waking/awakening.

By doing this process I was changing. I was transforming. I noticed that my Tarot readings for others were changing. During a reading for a friend I could just look at a card, and because I was using my intuitive muscles regularly by journeying with the cards, I would have an instant feeling of what the card was about, by remembering what its meaning was and what its message was for me. As such I had learnt from this and could pass my learnings onto others, helping them to see things differently.

This impacted not only on my readings for others, but also on readings for myself. I could read my own Tarot pack competently, but I could also read other Tarot decks too. All I had to do was to look at the card and I had a rough idea of what the card was telling me. This was fabulous in that I was feeling brave enough to work with complicated decks that I was previously fearful of like The Crowley Deck, or The Witches Tarot. The imagery did not need to be so basic as I was no longer just using my physical eye, but my intuitive eye too. I was also starting through the cards, to understand life, people, situations, and the Tarot in a much more profound way.

It was a huge awakening.

I was becoming the Hanged Man from the Major Arcana, I was seeing things from a different perspective. I had a greater insight, no longer was I seeing things one dimensional from a place of fear and judgement, but from a place of inner knowing as each Tarot card told me the story of life. This was crazy, but oh so very powerful. The cards were speaking to me in a way that was not obtainable from any Guru's Tarot book. There were no books that tapped straight into your intuition like a life injection. I was making my own book, the book on intuitive Tarot reading.

As my confidence grew, I started to work with a new advanced spread called "The Celtic Cross" (you can find this at the back of this book). This spread gave me a means to find out specifics in a reading, for example the personality, hopes and fears, and the future of whoever I was reading for. If during a reading, I did not remember the meaning of the card, or I started to lack confidence, I knew that I could turn to my very own book of meanings, showing each journey and then relay that message to the person I was reading for. Or see it as a direct trigger.

I continued with this intuitive Tarot reading process for many years, working as a fortune teller, a Tarot card reader. I read for friends and family looking at affairs of the heart, work, and other matters of life. I was busy as a Tarot reader, but something was missing, something lacked depth. I was finding my readings shallow, I was starting to find I was becoming more and more tired after readings. I was attracting in people that were needy. My readings were repetitive, always looking at the enquirers' relationships, answering such questions as "We have split up, when will he be back?" and "I am having an affair with a married man, he will leave his wife won't he?" and with each question, the reading was changing me. I was becoming cynical with each needy desperate client rapping at my heart strings. I was no longer delivering my readings with love, but with dysfunctionality. I was perceiving people as needy and dysfunctional. I did not see that they in fact needed help and love. My readings were not coming from a place of love, and I could sense the enquirers lacking love too. The majority of my clients were women. They were at a point where they were desperate in life with no sense of direction, no sense of their own inner empowerment or self-worth.

Don't get me wrong, I wanted to help people and to listen to them, but I was lacking in understanding, not knowing what was causing their unhappiness, and also lacking the tools to help them. I had the Tarot and my own intuition, but I needed more. I lacked understanding and empathy.

Susanna Dark

The Intuitive Tarot reading process had worked for me and I had a greater understanding, but I still felt that I needed to find out more. The Tarot had taught me about life. I had created my own Tarot book, but something was still missing.

I knew that there had to be more to being a Tarot reader, and I knew that I had to find a way in helping these people find themselves, to become the people that they used to be, the people that they should be. That is the beautiful beings of love they once were, before the affair with the married man started, before they got into the dysfunctional relationship. I needed to know more and to discover a greater empathy. I knew that the intuitive system had opened me up, ready for the next part of my journey. But where did I go next? Where and how did I take this process further?

# CHAPTER 4

## Time for Change

Back In 2006, my partner Dark and I relocated to Glastonbury in Somerset. We had loved this strange and powerful place for many years, so with no ties we moved, embarking on a new adventure. It was literally a fool's journey, as when we moved, neither of us had work planned for when we arrived, only our savings. We trusted that work would be there for us. I would take anything. Our need for change was that great.
We knew that we needed to leave London. Neither of us were happy. Dark had been through a very challenging personal time in his life, and I was bored in a mundane, normal job. My circle of friends had recently closed down with people moving away or leaving my life as part of the natural organic process of life. I knew, intuitively that this was the right time to move. I had no fear in my heart, purely excitement. I felt instinctively that Glastonbury was the way forwards for me. For us. I knew it was a place of miracles.
I knew that to start I would have to take on a mundane job, but I had a feeling that something else would follow, and initially I did a very "normal" job working in Morrisons. But then in 2007, in addition to my every day job, I started to read the Tarot at a psychic fair held in The Assembly Rooms. Initially I enjoyed working as a reader at this fair, but then, in 2008, I was spotted by Lindsay who owned the shop Yin Yang in Glastonbury High Street, and she asked me to work with her as a reader. I would be working self-employed, renting a room

in the therapy centre upstairs from her shop, working alongside healers and other readers, who also had rented rooms.

I would now be able to give up my mundane job! I could work as many days as I wished as a professional reader and I would publicise myself as such. I was ready. I had by now been reading for friends and family for over 13 years. I was able to conduct readings as a Tarot reader and fortune teller. For entertainment purposes only. This was the correct term that needed to be used for legal purposes.

Working at Yin Yang was a huge learning curve. The other readers consisted at the time of Gordon Strong, a successful master of the Tarot and author. Gordon was a lovely man, quietly spoken, with an inner sense of magick and confidence. One of the mediums that practiced at Yin Yang was Steven Jewell. Steve was a gifted medium, who specialised in healing, incorporating Seichem and Reiki into his practices. Again, a very gifted reader and healer.

Working with these professional gifted people, helped me to fine tune my readings and I was gaining a reputation for being an excellent reader myself.

On one occasion I remember a lady coming to see me for a reading. She sat down, and after I had finished with my introductory general reading, tuning into her and conveying what I had seen about her and her life, I asked her what she specifically wished to look at today in her reading. She then went on to tell me that she wished to look at her husband. Recently she had been in a car crash, had died very briefly and had to be resuscitated by the paramedics. It turned out that her husband had rigged the breaks on her car in order to cause her death.

The lady wanted to know what she should do. She did not want to prosecute her husband because she loved him, but she could not let him get away with such a horrendous act.

I think that as she was speaking my mouth was becoming bigger and bigger, and dropping to the floor, in shock! I never did discover what happened next…..
Glastonbury always attracted in the unusual story or unusual client.
It is a very powerful and magickal place to work, but due to the fact that it is built on magickal ley lines, it is also a very challenging place to work. It brings both miracles and nightmares in the extreme.

As my time at Yin Yang progressed I wanted to impart my knowledge as a teacher as well as a reader. I decided to hold one to one teachings at Yin Yang on Intuitive Tarot reading. These teachings would be for those interested in learning the Tarot from a different perspective. From an intuitive perspective.

Working alongside readers and healers introduced me to the alternative therapists that lived and worked in Glastonbury. It made me see the other side of life, the life of the professional therapist, and as such it must have brushed off on me, because I wanted to find out more about healing. But not just to work as a traditional healer, but how to incorporate healing into my readings. I had seen how powerful Reiki healing could be, but I wondered if healing could take place just as powerfully using only the process of a Tarot reading. What could I do and say that would heal a client?
I wanted to take my readings to another level. I would no longer just read as a Tarot reader, I would connect intuitively, looking deeper, using my form of intuitive reading. I would harness the power of the Tarot to transform using the images of the Tarot and communication. I would use it to deliver healing with understanding, empathy and compassion. This could not be found in a book, this needed to be found in life experience. To truly heal another, one must be empathetic rather than merely sympathetic. One cannot just pretend to understand the client, one must truly understand the client, empathically and intuitively.

Susanna Dark

I knew that if I understood healing from a place of empathy, I could really help my clients. I could find a way of combining what I had learnt during the intuitive process along with empathy and educate my clients to help them see things from a different perspective. Then, a great sense of healing could happen. This would be a totally different type of reading to what was being offered by the average fortune teller.

I had noticed that a lot of my clients were coming back to me again and again with the same questions. Nothing was happening to them after the reading. They were not learning or transforming. But what if I could offer a reading where change could occur. An alchemical process. If all could understand themselves, they could grow as people and start to self heal, and as such heal others? By connecting intuitively and by looking within, I knew that this was the way. The key.

From conducting readings from a face to face perspective, I then began conducting telephone readings too, working for one of the most successful celebrity psychics, via the psychic phone lines. You know the ones I mean, you see them advertised in the back of magazines. This was also a learning curve.

To work as a reader on a psychic telephone line involved logging onto a central phone system and being issued with a pin number. You were now no longer a name but a number. Clients would have the option to pay the company, via premium rate at roughly £1.50 per minute, or via credit card at around £45 for a half an hour call. The readers themselves earnt 35p per minute.

This was a very interesting experience. Customers that would call the premium rate number just wanted a fast fix. They wanted to know everything within five minutes to get their monies' worth. The most challenging part was that if a premium rate caller called you, and either did not rate you as a reader, or received the information that they needed straight away, they would slam the phone down, shocking you, and impacting on you in such a way that it immediately took away any confidence that you had. Readers are sensitive creatures and this was not a pleasurable experience in the slightest.

You can imagine the quality of the caller and the call for the premium rate number. The energetics of this option were not good, and as such would attract a different type of call and reading. That which I did not enjoy. This premium rate service was attracting in a client who was becoming addicted to the service, and as such it was making them unhealthy and needy. It was a five-minute fix.

The calls that were my favourite were those that called and paid the company via credit card. These were the professional clients that knew what they wanted to talk about. They understood how the readers worked, and as such had respect for the reader they were talking to, and the company itself. They had allocated time in their busy lives to consult a professional reader for guidance over an issue where they wanted to make changes. They had invested their money wisely and were taking the whole process seriously. It was a two-way process between the reader and the caller, and as such both benefitted.

Sometimes if a premium rate call came through I would put down the receiver as soon as the "Premium Rate" Voice indicator came through. So much I detested these premium rate calls.

I had my regulars, and I worked for the psychic lines on and off for over five years. It gave me great grounding and learning in how to read with integrity and professionalism.

When I had gained my confidence, on the phone lines. I started to conduct my own telephone readings from home. I found that a lot of clients were confused as to how I could conduct a reading for them, without both of us being in the same room, and I explained that using my gift and the Tarot, I

Susanna Dark

could connect to them, almost telepathically, and that having them sit physically across from me was not needed, or so I thought. I was later to experience, through client preference, that actually what was needed and what my clients preferred, was face to face readings. My clients needed to see me, to feel my contact, to see that I cared, and that I brought them hope. They needed that connection of love. They needed personalisation and to feel that special half an hour or hour of reading was dedicated to them and them only.

I had clients come to see me telling me that they needed to talk, just talk about their lives because they had nowhere else to go.
Whereas in the past you could visit your GP and talk to them, because of time constraints these days it was generally a quick session with drugs dispensed if necessary or a referral. There was no longer any type of deep healing, only a sticking plaster
There was no longer any sense of empathy, and as such no love.
People were feeling that no one cared about them, and that there was no understanding. No one had time for them.
When people are sick they are demonstrating in some way that they are lacking love. To be able then to go and see someone who could understand them with empathy would be the key to regaining this love.

To move onto this second stage though I needed to find out more. What causes illness? I knew that to be able to understand healing
I needed to understand the workings of illness. What causes it and also to look at some common types of illness. I needed to find out what was going on in the minds of these clients that I had who were in negative relationships, that had no self worth and were lacking in confidence. And then I had to find out how I could help them. And I meant REALLY help them.

Susanna Dark

I knew that I no longer wanted to work as a fortune teller. I wanted to become an alchemist. I wanted to help transform a client, by using a combination of the Tarot, my own intuition, and empathy. I started to explain to clients that I worked as such, and that if I was to read for them they genuinely needed to open up to the idea. I knew I needed to work with clients that genuinely needed help, not just the repetition of a session with a fortune teller. They needed an Intuitive, someone who could really bring forth transformation. I needed these clients to be open minded to all and to really want to change their lives.

Firstly though, more research was needed. I started to find the information that I needed online.

# Chapter 5

## What is illness?

Well if you go by the dictionary meaning, it means: - noun: illness; plural noun: illnesses - a disease or period of sickness affecting the body or mind - "he died after a long illness"

Illness is a state of mind.

The mind manifests a series of symptoms showing in the mind or body. Illnesses are quite often a catalyst telling us that something in our life needs to change, and this can be a situation, an outlook on life, or a perception of ourselves.

A catalyst is a person or situation, that appears to be negative at the time, but when we look back and after acceptance, it brings with it the greatest blessing. A catalyst is a huge life manifestation which can often come through as illness, redundancy, an accident, an affair, or something equally dramatic.

We all need to embrace change, it is essential in life, but due to our fear of the future, we block the flow of energy that we have within to bring forth the change and instead it creates a stagnant dark blockage, manifesting in the form of illness.

## Psychosomatic Illness

The meaning of the word Psychosomatic means mind (psyche) and body (soma).

A psychosomatic disorder is a disease which involves both mind and body.

Some physical diseases are thought to be particularly prone to be made worse by mental factors such as stress and anxiety.

What actually causes the illnesses and diseases we suffer?

Illness is caused by imbalance. An imbalance of the mind brought on by a series of factors.

The Guru Deepak Chopra says. *"Most people assume that germs and genes cause disease. The germ theory has brought us a long way, and genetic theory promises to take us even further. But there is still a mystery surrounding why certain people get sick while others don't.*

*For example, studies show that if cold virus is placed directly into a person's nose, the chance of getting a cold is about 1 in 8; being exposed to chill, damp, or a draft doesn't increase these odds. Also, when the Black Death wiped out a third of Europe's population in the 14th century, no one knows why the other two-thirds, who were certainly exposed, didn't die.*

*Every day each of us inhales or ingests enough germs to cause a variety of diseases we never contract. Some sort of "control by the host" seems to be at work. This refers to the body's ability to live with disease-causing agents without getting sick. Germs aren't the only factor.*

*Statistics show that severely ill people often wait until a significant date has passed, such as Christmas or their birthday, before suddenly dying.*

*Studies going back to the Korean War showed that young soldiers in their early twenties had serious blockage of their coronary arteries, yet the disease doesn't show up until middle age.*

*Not everyone exposed to HIV contracts the virus, and in a few rare instances, those with AIDS have reversed their viral status from positive to negative.*

*Why, then, would you or I get sick when someone else equally at risk
doesn't?*

*The best way to get sick is to suffer from as many of the following conditions as possible:*

- *Unsanitary conditions: massive exposure to germs remains a major factor.*

- *Being poor: poverty degrades life on all fronts, including health.*

- *High stress: physical and psychological stress damage the immune system.*

- *Depression and anxiety: untreated psychological disorders weaken resistance to a wide range of diseases, perhaps even cancer*

- *Lack of coping mechanisms: stress by itself is a negative factor, but the inability to bounce back from it is more important*

- *Lack of control, victimization: all stresses become much worse if you feel that you have no control over your own life.*

- *Inertia, sedentary lifestyle: if you are inactive and have no outside interests, your chance of getting sick rises sharply*

- *Feeling alone and unloved: emotional deprivation is as unhealthy as deprivation of good food.*

- *Sudden loss: the sudden loss of a job or spouse, a reversal in finances, or finding yourself in the midst of a war or natural disaster all constitute a state of loss and lead to higher risk of getting sick.*

- *Growing old: once considered a major cause of illness, aging is now known not to be a direct cause. Being healthy into your eighties should be your expectation, but if you neglect yourself in old age, the body becomes vastly more susceptible to disease.*

*None of these factors comes as a huge surprise, since public health officials have drummed into us that most illness in modern society is a "lifestyle disease" born of stress, lack of exercise, and other factors external to germs. But I think most people still assume that being fat, for example, is worse for you than stress, which certainly isn't the case. Outside of diabetes and joint problems, it's hard to find a serious link between moderate overweight and any disorder, while stress and its offshoots are major risks and exaggerate the effect of ageing. Yet in the absence of high blood pressure and artery disease, most people will live a very long time, probably in good health until they contract their final illness. (I've covered a dozen other common beliefs, both true and false, in earlier posts recently.) But the mystery of who specifically gets sick remains unsolved, in part because there are subtle factors that few experts have adequately examined.*

- *Some people get sick because they expect to.*

- *Some people get sick, or sicker, after they are diagnosed with a disease.*

- *Disease brings certain benefits, known as "secondary gains," that make it positive. The classic example is a child who pretends to be sick in order to get more love and attention, but adults find secondary gains of their own, such as not having to take responsibility for their lives or finding an escape from a situation they can't cope with.*

- *Some people get sick because they want to give up, or even die.*

- *Some people have nothing better to do than to get sick."*

We are all aware of the everyday illnesses that we are exposed to. We experience these or are aware of friends or family members that are experiencing them or have done in the past. But how many of us actually know the cause of these illnesses? I have always been fascinated with what goes on in people's minds, and what may or may not have triggered the illness, and why they experienced it at a particular time in their lives. I have always been a creature that questioned life and never accepted that it had to be the way that it is. I am a mover and a shaker, a creature (as sometimes seen by others!) of disharmony.

I knew that in life you should be aware of what is in your mind and what you feed your belly. So, I knew that as our thoughts could manifest illness, what we eat can create it too.

Deepak Chopra says *"By becoming self-aware, you gain ownership of reality; in becoming real, you become the master of both inner and outer life."*

By being aware of what food we put in our bodies, by being aware of what we think and what we say and that all this has power in our lives, then we can start to change and bring about that change.
Once we are aware of our thought patterns we can also challenge our beliefs. I don't mean from a religious

perspective, but from a confidence perspective. To illustrate, an example of a belief in others is:

"I believe that my children are going to achieve at school. I have the utmost confidence in them."

Some negative beliefs that you hold about yourself could be:

"I am a bad person. I do not do enough for others."

"I am useless at my job. I am not getting anywhere. I believe I shall fail."

"I am a bad wife. I never seem to do enough for my husband or family."

If you hold these beliefs as being true, then you give them power, power over your life and you. I am not asking you to try and be perfect as this in itself is illusion, but when you have a thought such as this, correct it. For example, say to yourself "I am not a bad person. I try my best and treat others as I would expect to be treated myself. I know I shall endeavour to learn and grow." Every time you have a negative thought that disempowers you, turn it around, and find the words that would help you to improve your life and be happier. This process is called finding "Positive Affirmations".

If you spend your days wallowing in regrets about the past or fears of the future, you will most likely see more worries appearing. Our minds are powerful things, able to create miracles. In life we have to achieve balance. I am not going to say banish all negative thoughts from your mind. They do have a purpose in that they help us to bring about change, if we acknowledge them for what they are, just part of a process. When a negative thought comes to you acknowledge it. Understand that this is telling you that something needs to change. Then you will see it for what it is, and not a thing to be feared.

Every single thought that you have is a "thing". Our thoughts are made from matter, so they really DO matter. If you think positively, you will attract positive in. If you think negatively this is the case also. It is called the Boomerang Effect. Becoming mindful of your own thoughts helps you to see what you should keep or remove from your own mind.

Triggers can take the form of internal thoughts or spoken words, but they can also be represented visually. You can mouth in the mirror " I am going to have a good day", or you can pop a sticky note on the bathroom cabinet or fridge saying, " Everything is going to be ok." These are just triggers to give us peace, to help us calm down and get control of a situation.You can even write a trigger down and then leave it by the bed side for the morning. A good one to write is, "Today I shall take each step at a time" or, "I am happier than I think I am". All I am saying is that you can try and look at your thoughts, about yourself and others, and try to change them. It really is that simple.

We are more powerful and magikcal then we think we are.

## Negative thoughts, moods and behaviours

We all have negative moods. Mine are often caused by my hormones. Perhaps something has upset you earlier and you have not shifted from that time and are still carrying it with you. We can though become addicted to these moods. Who is prone to saying this?

" I love nothing better than a bit of drama."

" I love the fact that she craves attention, I find it all very entertaining."

These are all the things we say, our negative behaviour and the observation of others in life that we find funny. But should we find them funny, and are they are doing us more harm than good? How many of us love to indulge a good gossip now and again? It is so easy to judge others. But if only we were aware of the harm that we were doing to ourselves, the negativity that we were putting out that will eventually come back to us as a boomerang. This negative form of thinking is going to really hurt no one other than ourselves and is stopping us from being totally happy.

"Oh Sue, it's just a bit of fun." we say, but really? Thoughts are things. Are we being lazy and negative in our thinking? Do we relax more in our ways of thinking than we should do? If we watch what we eat for our diet, should we not watch what we think too? Body and mind are inextricably linked. I am not wanting you to become a robot, just to harness your own inner magick, to make you happier and stronger, and for your life to be different and more magickal than it is already.

I remember in 2017 when I went for surgery, my dear friend Elayne mentioned to me that if I go into surgery with a smile on my face, no matter how scared I might be, that I would recover more quickly. By changing my thought process and being in a happy place faster healing would come about, and I have to say it worked! Look at those who are forever ill. They do not have an illness, they have actually BECOME the illness. They have let this take over their lives due to fear. They are so used to thinking this way, that they think that to be ill is the norm. This is now their new identity and existence.

Susanna Dark

I want you to be conscious of the way that you think. Be aware now of what happens to these thoughts. Be aware that they seem to flow as you think. Now be aware of a negative thought, an inner fear that you may have, and suddenly see how your mind freezes. The thought has ceased flowing. If it is moving, it is moving backwards. If our thoughts are things as we said, then every action must have a reaction.

Yes, another example of the boomerang effect in action.

I want to give you an example of how powerful our thoughts are. Have you noticed that you may have said something to someone or done something and known at the time that it was wrong, but you did it anyway? The extreme feeling that you felt at the time, where you felt guilty, well that thought, that feeling of guilt has to go somewhere. You have put it out there and it has to come back as that boomerang. As with every action comes a reaction. Now this boomerang might come back immediately or the next day, but that extreme thought will come back to you, make no mistake.

These boomerangs can be viewed as lessons. Lessons to help us learn about ourselves and how we think. They help us to take responsibility for our thoughts and of ourselves, and to stop us from being and feeling the victim. They do not punish us but help us to understand that with every thought that we have, we create our lives.

We are given what we need, not what we want.

We can though, use the boomerang effect to our advantage. What if you want to change a situation fast? If you want a situation where you feel that you have been treated unfairly to change, well you can achieve this. As long as you have been truthful in your actions and words and done nothing wrong, this feeling of being treated unfairly can be improved upon. You can harness the power of thought, simply by putting the same amount of emotion into your anger at the misjustice that has been done to you. Do this either by shouting it out loud or writing it down. Then by putting extreme emotion and passion into your thoughts, firmly expressing your belief that it should be a certain way, (as long as you are coming from a place of truth), then you can change the situation. Try it, it really does work!

## Catalysts

A catalyst is a situation or person that brings great change into your life. This catalyst occurs because we are too lazy or fearful to bring about the change naturally ourselves. Here is an example of this.
I remember years ago working in a job that was bringing great stress to my life. Not only was it against my beliefs, it was a tiring job. I was unappreciated, it was sexist, in fact totally dysfunctional. I took the job because the salary was good - end of story. I sold myself to the money. I hated the job and I hated my life.

Every day I would travel hours to and from work taking three buses in the process. I would have an early start to the day and then have to get to bed early to be able to function at all. This went on for months and it was making me so very miserable.
One day I had an accident. I was so tired after work that I tripped up and fell so hard that I ripped open both my knees and lost my front teeth. I had become physically weak due to this job. Weak in mind therefore weak in disposition. Change needed to happen. The catalyst needed to happen. I was not going to change my job, I was used to being miserable and suffering with the awful routine and job every day.

I was too stuck in my ways to bring about the change.

So, this catalyst needed to happen in order to bring about the change, and for the healing process to begin. As long as I recognised the catalyst for what it was. I was in a state of emotional illness and physical illness and a healing needed to take place. I needed to heal. I needed to embrace change.

### Removing the blame off others/Self Ownership

It is so easy to blame our stuff on others. We have had a bad day at work, and what do we do, we come home and shout at our partner. We say all the words that we are carrying within, about our life, and the way that we feel about ourselves. It is so easy to dump our stuff on others rather than taking ownership, and then making the changes we need to ourselves and our lives and in doing so achieving happiness. It is the lazy option.

If we are unhappy with work, then identify that we are unhappy. Can we change jobs? Can we meet with our boss and talk over our indifferences? If not, can we change our perspective on the way we see stuff? Can we sit, think and decide what subtle changes can be made?

An example of this is could be where we have an issue with someone, say for instance our boss. If we were to write down everything they had said that annoys us, could we then read it through, process it, and perhaps understand that person, and the message that they are trying to bring. If we are unable at the time to see this and feel that our boss is indeed at fault, could there be a hidden message? Could it be that it is in fact time for us to retire, or look for another job but we are just not admitting this to ourselves. We may have been thinking recently how tired we have been, and that we have wished we had more time to do what we wanted but have pushed these thoughts to the back of our minds. Remember that thoughts are things and that they do have power. Be careful what you think and what you wish for!

By looking into things more deeply, but changing our thought processes, we can become self-empowered and self-aware. So…. stop, breathe, think and then act. Take ownership of your thoughts and your lives.

## Emotional shut down

From the article on the journey website, they say that 85% of our illnesses are emotionally based.

*"This research strongly suggests that in the long run, suppressing or avoiding our instinctive emotional responses to life's challenges adversely affects our health. To put things very simply, when an emotion is triggered in us, releasing a natural biochemistry into our bodies and we allow ourselves to fully feel the emotion, then it along with the associated chemicals washes through our body, usually quite quickly, leaving no residue.*

*But when we are emotionally triggered and we shut down, suppress or avoid the experience and our true feelings the result is very different. The released chemicals associated with the emotion remain in our bloodstream and subsequently the residue gets stored inside our bodies. Over time, if illness is going to happen, it will likely occur in these places where the chemical residues are stored.*

*Numerous scientists and medical doctors have studied and subsequently verified research supporting this. US scientist Candace B. Pert, Ph.D., in particular, has compellingly shown that suppressing emotions can lead to specific cell receptors in our bodies becoming blocked.*

*These blocks then compromise the normal healthy communications between cells, impairing many bodily functions, weakening our normal immune responses and potentially creating illness."*

This brings to mind an example of a work colleague who had lost a dear friend to cancer.

Fiona had been talking about a friend of hers who was dying from terminal cancer. Causes of death also fascinated me and I asked Fiona what in her opinion could have been the trigger and if she felt that there could have been one. She told me that shortly before her friend was diagnosed with terminal cancer, that this friend's father had died. This had obviously been a very challenging time for the whole family, and Fiona believed that the shock of his death had been the trigger. Then tragically, both Fiona's friend and her friend's mother were diagnosed with cancer at the same time, and they both died two years after diagnosis.

The emotional trigger of losing a husband and father, the pain of keeping their emotions contained, perhaps unable to show this immense pain due to emotional upbringing or fear of being judged, or perhaps sheer delay in grieving, meant that this pain had to manifest itself in another way. This time it manifested itself as cancer.

Another example is in a friend of mine, Mike. Mike had a very closed persona emotionally, and I remember instantly feeling a sense of dislike when I first met him. I had no reason as to why I felt as I did, as I did not know him, but I knew intuitively that something was wrong from an emotional perspective. I felt that he was carrying something from the past within him, a self-judgement or pain that he had not released. I wondered if I was in some way, tuning into the dislike that he felt for himself, as Mike was prone to self-judgement. I remember feeling that he carried an inner rigidity and was not able to be himself or communicate as he might have wanted in some way. This again, could have been due to a rigid upbringing, and I often think of the repetition that happens in families, where a parent or parents find it difficult to show love or openly communicate, so that in some instances, it shows up in how their children are with their own children and so on.

A couple of years later Mike was diagnosed with cancer, but he managed to pull through and recover. Luckily, he is now in remission and a totally different person emotionally with a positive outlook on life. He is now more open and able to discuss all matters freely.
I wonder if this cancer was a catalyst too and, in some way changed Mike's life so that he saw himself, his life and others differently. I wonder if it was a shock tactic, brought by an unseen hand of fate but delivered with love, not judgement. Food for thought maybe, but to some, an idea that will be hard to take on board.

Could cancer lie dormant in the body, like a time bomb waiting for a trigger? Or only become active when an emotional or physical blockage is created by stagnant energy?

When my mother lost my sister Angela, back in the 1970's due to heart failure, she found comfort in food and started to gain a lot of weight and is now a type 2 diabetic.

The loss of a child is a terrible thing that you never get over.
A year later my mother decided to have another child and my brother James was brought into the world. However, she did not realise that to have another child, (in a lot of cases) does not repair a hole, the void created by bereavement. So, she took to eating food to try and fill that void and is now overweight and medically classified as obese.
This was/is emotional suffering, caused by the bereavement.

My father has suffered with mental illness all his life. As I described earlier growing up in a home environment that was far from ideal created in my father's mind a desire to seek out perfection as a way of escaping from the imperfections of his life.

He married my mother, the perfect, blonde, slim woman that she was then, perceiving in his mind that she was the perfect woman. She was not perfect of course, blessed with the normal flaws of humanity. When he came to realise this, as all perfection is illusion, he could not deal with it. Again, another example of my father craving faultlessness.

This desire to seek out the unreal created a sense of inner anxiety and depression that he still carries today. When my sister passed over my father refused to go for counselling. He took her death as a lot of parents would do, from a place of self-judgement. He felt he had caused her death and in his mind he was the murderer. My father had created something that was not perfect, so he had wished it away.

At this time my father was working in a high-powered, stress-filled job, totally unsuitable for his sensitive demeanour.

This stopped his natural flow of thought. His mind was rigid, and over stressed with an emotional blockage, and this in turn caused a mental breakdown.

Another form of emotional shut down can be found with elderly couples that have been married for many years. It is almost as though their souls form as one. They entwine energetically, and it is very common that when one passes over, the other follows them shortly after. In many instances it can be of heart failure due to a broken heart. The loss of their best friend, soul mate and life's companion is too much to bear. Like a type of entwined twin, one goes then the other must follow. In this case, this is death of the mind, body and spirit.

**Exercises using The Tarot to help heal emotional shutdown.**

We have looked at various examples of people that have suffered some sort of emotional shutdown. Now we must look at how we might help them to heal using the Tarot as a tool. Which card/cards would you choose to help them and why?

For the purpose of easy reading the client in these exercises will be referred to in the feminine.

I suggest that for this exercise we choose from the Major Arcana only.
I myself would select The Empress card. The reasoning behind selecting The Empress as the card for healing is that it represents the mother, the emotionally abundant character of the Major Arcana. To connect to this card is to reconnect to your own inner power of healing, love and abundance. To almost go back into the womb of life and be reborn for to be reborn is then to be healed. If my client was to meditate on this card, using the process described I feel that she would find an inner sense of realisation and transformation. She would discover an inner knowing of what needs to be done to be able to move forwards in life. She will be creating her own book of meanings.

Now you have a think as to which card you might use and add to your notebook.

Now to a three card Tarot reading. Ask the powers of the Tarot themselves, "How is it possible to heal my client from an emotional shutdown?"

Shuffle the cards and as you shuffle, close your eyes, still your mind, and ask the Tarot, "What are the cards for emotional shut down". It is as easy as this. The more direct and clear your question is, the clearer the answer will be. Then select the three cards off the top of the deck.

So, let's say I have conducted a three-card reading on emotional shutdown, and these are the cards that came off the top of the pack.

***The Past - Wheel Of Fortune***
***Present - The Sun***
***Future - The Devil.***

Now remember I am using my own meanings from the intuitive journey that I have made with each card. I can refer back to the notebook of my meanings at any time if needed.

From the cards that I have selected it tells me that the client has had emotional illness in the past, she is prone to this (The wheel of fortune). This is because she often hides behind a mask of illusion, (The Sun), instead of being the true person that she is, due to her sensitivity. For the future (The Devil) she may have to deal with further challenges, but to see this, as part of a break through, and that all is relevant, for us to grow and become a stronger person. I now feel intuitively, and you can do this too, that I want to deal one more card. I am listening to my intuition.

I have dealt the Hermit and this tells me that my client will need to spend some time looking within and do some soul searching, to be able to find herself and her direction. But this CAN be achieved. To look within is not a place of fear, but a place of discovery and healing.

Now you do exactly the same process and write your findings in your notebook. If you do not know someone that you can base your reading on, ask, "How would I heal someone who is experiencing an emotional shutdown?"

## Physical illness

What I mean by physical illness is bodily injury, headache, or any other physical impairment. Life is a stressful thing in today's society. Women are expected to do more than ever before. In the past women were the bearers of the children, they were the stay at home mothers, looking after the children, their husband and the house. As women today, we are expected to do so much more. Not only do we bear the roles of the past, but we are also expected, in a lot of households to go to work too. Quite often there is no choice because of financial burdens.

Men are expected to work longer hours in order to support their partners and family. And they must also look after the children, for if their wives are working and an emergency occurs, they must jump into action as a support factor for child and mother.
Society has created huge expectations for us. We are expected to get married, raise children, have expensive housing, have the latest mod cons and live to a certain standard as dictated by advertisers. It is a society built on judgement and negativity. We are given unrealistic demands and expectations. This puts stress on our minds, and as such, our bodies too.

When we are stressed out in life it shows in our bodies. We carry the stress in our bodies. If you have a pain in the neck, this can literally mean that something or someone is a "Pain in the neck" and as such we carry the stress in this area.
We carry stress in our faces, and that can often be shown in our expressions. We have dark circles under our eyes. Perhaps we have lost weight due to stress, and it shows in our faces in the lines and the lack of skin tone. A lot of physical illness can be caused by anxiety and depression; a manifestation of these mental illnesses.

Headaches are in some instances caused by dehydration, but a lot of the time they are caused by stress, the stresses of life that we are battling to deal with due to emotional fears and blockages.

(I have included in the exercise section at the end of the book, a simple meditation for unwinding and relaxing, to alleviate the stresses of the day or week)

## Exercises using the Tarot to help heal physical illness.

If you could help someone to heal from a physical illness using the Tarot as a tool which card/cards would you choose to help someone who had experienced a physical illness, and why?
I suggest that for this exercise we choose from the Major Arcana only.

I would suggest that they meditate with The Strength card, to understand that to bear all in life on our own and not asking for help is not a sign of strength but of weakness. It is much better for us to learn to share our load, and to accept that not being able to cope is not a sign of weakness but of being human.

Now you have a think as to which card you would use and add to your notebook.

I shall now shuffle the cards and as I shuffle I shall ask in my mind "What are the cards to help physical illness". It is as easy as this. The more direct and clear the question, the clearer the reading. Again, I am using the Major Arcana only. I will now select the three cards off the top of the deck, to conduct a three-card reading.

**The past - The Star**
**Present - The Illusion**
**Future - The Sun**

Now remember I am using my meanings, from the journey that I have made with each card. I can refer back to the notebook of my meanings if I need to.

When I look to the Star, I see the hopes and dreams we aspire to in life, but looking at the Illusion card, I know that sometimes these are purely fantasies and not realistic aspirations. We can, at times find it hard to identify what is real and what is illusion. Do not set yourself unrealistic goals. Look to the simple pleasures in life (the Sun) and be happy. Live life every day as it comes. Know that to connect to your inner child of happiness within is the key.

Now you do exactly the same process and write your findings in your notebook. If you do not know someone that you can base your reading on ask, "How would I heal someone with a physical illness?"

## Mental illness

I was born witness to mental illness from an early age. I was eight years old when my sister died of two holes in her heart. Shortly after that my father had a series of mental breakdowns. These mental breakdowns not only affected him, but my mother also. People do not realise how mental illness impacts on all those around. In my father's case, the way in which he handled or did not handle his illness would be to sit in front of the newspaper, day in day out, and say nothing. He would just stare at the newspaper. (Thinking more on this, I wonder if he was craving the perfection of his childhood, and the hidden memory of his uncle's newspaper). He did not wish to communicate with anyone, and in the end my mother set fire to the paper to get some sort of reaction from him. The extreme upset, isolation and confusion that this illness brought to my father and mother was obvious.
Shortly after this, my father went to visit his GP, who put him on medication. He was diagnosed with depression.
Depression is a disease that can be hereditary, and in my family's case, my father has passed this depression onto both my brothers. Luckily this has not come to me.

## Anxiety

My husband suffers from anxiety and depression. He needs to have routine is his life, and he needs to know that all is as it is, and the same every day, or he starts to feel that himself and his life are out of control. Anxiety can be triggered by a past event. On the NHS Website, Anxiety is explained as this.

"Anxiety can bring on physical symptoms. Anxiety is a feeling of unease, such as worry or fear, that can be mild or severe."

Everyone has feelings of anxiety at some point in their lives, for example, you may feel worried and anxious about sitting an exam or having a medical test or job interview. During times like these, feeling anxious can be perfectly normal. However, some people find it hard to control their worries. Their feelings of anxiety are more constant and can often affect their daily lives. Anxiety is the main symptom of several conditions, including panic disorder, phobias such as agoraphobia, or claustrophobia, post-traumatic stress disorder or social anxiety disorder.

**Exercises using the Tarot to help heal Anxiety.**

Which card/cards would you choose to help someone who had experienced anxiety and why? I suggest that for this exercise we choose from the Major Arcana only.

I would suggest that they meditate with The Sun card, to understand that to try and live each day in the moment is the key to happiness. To understand that you are safe at all times. Try and work with the "Happy Place" meditation listed in this book. Look at your own limitations, and do not judge yourself. To force yourself to behave in a particular way and to set yourself unrealistic expectations could make matters worse. Understand that everyone has their faults in life and that you are not alone. The Sun will help you to connect to your inner child, and that by finding a way to have fun and to play, it will help you to start to heal.

Now you have a think as to which card you would use and add to your notebook.

I shall now shuffle the cards, and as I shuffle I shall ask in my mind "What are the cards to help someone with Anxiety?" as straight forward as this. The more direct and clear the question, the clearer the reading. Again, I am using the Major Arcana only. I select the three cards off the top of the deck to conduct the three-card reading..

**The Past – Mastery (The Chariot)**
**Present - Strength**
**Future - The World**

Again, remember I am using my intuitive meanings, from the journey that I have made with each card. I can always refer back to the notebook of my meanings if I need to.

I can see from the past that the client has battled with indecision. There was a time in her life when she did not feel in a place of security (The Chariot) and did not know her direction. This has brought on a sense of vulnerability. To be able to cope (Strength) with this, she needs to focus on her hidden strength, and a new way of thinking. When I look to her future, I see that this sense of anxiety may continue to be present in life, (The World) but that through connecting to her inner strength, she will be able to cope with it better.

If I were choosing cards for a client to journey with, I would suggest the following three cards.
1. The Fool (To embrace a new beginning, and a new way of thinking) 2. The Emperor (They may decide to seek out a therapist, or counsellor to help)
3. Karma ( To find the peace that they crave and to discover a new understanding of themselves and their life.)

If my client were to meditate on these cards, I feel that they would find an inner sense of realisation, and transformation, an inner knowing of what they need to do intuitively to be able to move forwards in their life. They will be creating their own book of meanings.

Susanna Dark

Now you do exactly the same process and write your findings in your notebook. If you do not know someone that you can base your reading on, ask, "How would I heal someone with anxiety?"

**Depression** (Again, from the NHS website)

"There is no single cause of depression. It can occur for a variety of reasons and it has many different triggers. For some people, an upsetting or stressful life event, such as bereavement, divorce, illness, redundancy and job or money worries, can be the cause. Different causes can often combine to trigger depression. For example, you may feel low after being ill and then experience a traumatic event, such as a bereavement, which brings on depression. People often talk about a "downward spiral" of events that leads to depression. For example, if your relationship with your partner breaks down, you're likely to feel low, you may stop seeing friends and family and you may start drinking more. All of this can make you feel worse and trigger depression. Some studies have also suggested that you're more likely to get depression as you get older, and that it's more common in people who live in difficult social and economic circumstances.

**Exercises using the Tarot to help heal Depression.**

If you could help someone to heal from depression using the Tarot as a tool which card/cards would you choose to help someone who had experienced depression, and why? I suggest that for this exercise we choose from the Major Arcana only.
I would suggest that they meditate with The Fool card, to understand that to create and plan and manifest is important. Start a new project, something as simple as sorting out a wardrobe or a chest of drawers. Suggest they make a list of things to do. Distraction would be an appropriate solution as brooding on one's thoughts can be the pathway to depression.

Now you have a think as to which card you would use and add to your notebook.

I shall now shuffle the cards and as I shuffle I shall ask in my mind "What are the cards to help someone with depression?" as easy as this. The more direct and clear the question, the clearer the reading. Again, I am using the Major Arcana only. I then deal the three cards from the top of the deck.

**Past –     Mastery – (The Chariot)**
**Present -  Strength**
**Future -   The Wise One (The Hermit)**

Now again remember I am using my meanings, from the journey that I have made with each card and can refer back to the notebook of my meanings if needed.

When I look to the past of my client I can see a time of indecision and a time of confusion. There was a journey, but it did not go as planned (Mastery). Now she knows she must be strong and is dealing with life in the best way possible, and deals with it, at present, by wearing that face of bravado (Strength). However, in the future I see she may not be able to keep face, but if she searches deep to find courage and a trust that the challenging time is for a reason, then her own inner wisdom (The Wise One) will come through, and she will become wiser as a result of these challenging times.

If I were choosing cards for a client to journey with I would suggest the following three cards:

 1. The Wise One – For inner wisdom, to gain insight.
 2. The Empress for self-love and inner nurturing
 3. The High Priestess, to look within and listen to your own intuition.

If my client was to meditate on these, I feel that she would find an inner sense of realisation, and transformation, an inner knowing of what she needs to do intuitively to be able to move forwards in her life. She will be creating her own book of meanings.

Now you do exactly the same process and write your findings in your notebook. If you do not know someone that you can base you reading on, ask "How would I heal someone with depression?"

## Food allergies/Anorexia and obesity

Today more and more people are experiencing so called "food allergies". Gluten, wheat, dairy, the list goes on. But what is really behind these allergies, and all other allergies? And are we really allergic to food, or is it life?

When I was a child we had a dog, and every day this dog would run up to me and knock me over. I was about three years old. This in turn created a fear of dogs, which in turn brought on asthma and a dog allergy. This was an illness brought on by fear. The cause of the asthma was not a dog allergy, but the fear associated by the dog. A fear of not being in control.

I have a friend called Mabel, and she has a number of food allergies.
She has had a very turbulent relationship with her mother which has brought on an inability to be able to relax and be herself.
Mabel needs to feel in control of herself, her life and her body, but as a very sensitive lady she is unable to do this at times. Mabel is sensitive to others, and to her environment. She is a caring soul, but is unable to nurture herself, only others.
When our lives feel empty, we find things that can fill it. In Mabel's case she has filled her life with food allergies. Instead of her allergies, and illness being part of her life, she has become her illness. She has become allergic to herself.

## Anorexia

I remember years ago my friend Anna being unable to eat. She was gradually becoming thinner and thinner by the day. Anna had been living with a flat mate, but they were socially incompatible. Anna had had issues with living with people in the past and also had anger issues from her own past. In effect she had issues with living with herself, never mind living with anyone else. So, Anna and her flat mate argued. Anna felt controlled, the flat mate left the arrangement, but this did not help the situation. Anna felt her issues resurfacing from the past, which created a mental block over food and her body image. Anna judged herself, which created a lack of self-love. This created anxiety and depression, and anorexia.

A little on Anorexia from the NHS website.

"Anorexia is an eating disorder and serious mental health condition. People who have anorexia try to keep their weight as low as possible by not eating enough food or exercising too much, or both. This can make them very ill because they start to starve. They often have a distorted image of their bodies, thinking they are fat even when they are underweight. Men and women of any age can get anorexia, but it's most common in young women and typically starts in the mid-teens.

## Obesity

In my opinion, as mentioned earlier in the case of my mother, obesity it is brought on by a lack of self-love, (wanting to feed others, to please them, and to fill an emotional void)
The listed cause on the NHS website is - "Obesity is generally caused by eating too much and moving too little. If you consume high amounts of energy, particularly fat and sugars, but don't burn off the energy through exercise and physical activity, much of the surplus energy will be stored by the body as fat."
That is the medical diagnosis. This however is from an emotional perspective as quoted on Ygoy.com

Susanna Dark

"Studies have found that some people eat more when affected by depression, anxiety, binge eating or other emotional disorders. Being overweight and obese is often the cause of these psychological disorders. It is a vicious cycle whereby the greater the emotions, conflicts and difficulties, the greater the incidence of unhealthy eating and obesity. It is commonly believed that some people overeat because of depression, hopelessness, anger, boredom and many other reasons that have nothing to do with hunger. It is also always not necessary that overweight and obese people have more emotional problems than other people. In fact, obese people are vulnerable to their feelings which influences their eating habits, causing them to overeat."

By getting into a negative pattern of eating, we can get used to eating as we do, unaware of our portion sizes, and find ourselves in a sense of denial.

**Exercises using the Tarot to help someone to heal who has an eating disorder.**

Which card/cards would you choose to help someone who is suffering from an eating disorder and why?
Again I suggest that for this exercise we choose from the Major Arcana only.

I would suggest that they meditate with The Guide card, as in some mental illnesses the person refuses to admit that they are ill and are unable to see the illness for what it is.

To be able to get the client to have hope and to trust in something greater than they are may help to give them belief in something other worldly, away from the unhappy life that they are in now, so that they can focus on this as a way of giving them strength. To some it may seem that I have suggested an unhealthy delusional substitute rather than encouraging the person to face their issues. But in some cases this is a subconscious way of working that will help them focus on the unseen, gaining inner strength that will then impact on their worldly lives, and the issue itself.

Now you have a think as to which card you would use and add to your notebook.

I shall now shuffle the cards, and as I shuffle I shall ask in my mind "What are the cards to help someone with an eating disorder?" as easy as this. The more direct and clear the question, the clearer the reading. Again, I am using the Major Arcana only. I then select the three cards off the top of the deck.

**Past -**     **The Wise One (The Hermit)**
**Present - The Empress**
**Future -**    **The High Priestess.**

Please remember I am using my meanings, from the journey that I have made with each card. I can refer back to the notebook of my meanings if needed.

I can see from the past that my client had to live her life from a place of wisdom and practicality (The Wise One). This was a time when fun and spontaneity was rare. Now she wants to be empowered, but it is a time for looking at self-love. When I look to the future I see a time where the past will make sense, where she can tap into her intuition, (The High Priestess) and understand that everything from the past has made her as she is today, with a sense of inner peace, and forgiveness of the past. She will then be able to embrace the empowerment she desires.

If I were choosing cards for a client to journey with I would suggest the following three cards.
1.The Sun (To connect to the inner child, and to have fun)
2.Karma (To achieve a greater understanding of their circumstances)

Susanna Dark

3. The Wise One (To be able to make practical choices and steps to move forwards)

If my client was to meditate on these, I feel that she would find an inner sense of realisation, and transformation, an inner knowing of what she needs to do intuitively to be able to move forwards in her life. She will be creating her own book of meanings.

Now you do exactly the same process and write your findings in your notebook. If you do not know someone that you can base you reading on, ask, "How would I help someone with an eating disorder?"

After I had investigated illness and wondered how it applied to my life and the ones that I loved I wanted to find out more. I was eager for knowledge. I wanted to find out why we heal others and look at self-healing. The more I was thinking and the more I was reading, the more I wanted to find out. The Tarot process had opened my mind.

# Chapter 6

## Why Do we Want to Heal Others/Self-Healing

By healing others we can also heal and help ourselves. When we start to understand what is causing our friends' and loved ones' illnesses and state of mind, we start to become empathetic.
We realise that love is the answer, and we reach out to love and heal.
By healing others we are reaching out and connecting to the Divine, with the hope that those we heal, will discover/rediscover the Divine within themselves; that the healing will create an opening.

To want to help another is to show love. We want those that we love to be happy and healthy. When those that we love are happy, we are happy.
The cause of illness is fear and the cure is love.
The period of personal growth leading to healing, can be called self-healing, self-awareness.

In Wikipedia self-healing is described as such: "Self-healing refers to the process of recovery (generally from psychological disturbances, trauma etc.), motivated by and directed by the patient, guided often only by instinct.. Such a process encounters mixed fortunes due to its amateur nature, although self-motivation is a major asset. The value of self-healing lies in its ability to be tailored to the unique experience and requirements of the individual. The process can be helped and accelerated with introspection techniques such as meditation"

With self-healing comes self-love. I do not mean from an ego perspective, in the way when you look in the mirror with false appreciation. I mean self-forgiveness and self-understanding. Self-love is being able to look at yourself warts and all and say "Hey I am not perfect, but I love you. I may have made some mistakes in the past, but I have learnt from them, and now I am able to let go. Because I understand that unless I do and I start to love myself from a place of self-acceptance, then how can I be happy and healthy? How can others love me, and how can I love and help others?"

Can you remember at the beginning of the book I talked about my mother and father, and how they have battled with their own challenges in life? I believe that we are all put on this planet to learn lessons so that we can grow and evolve. I do not believe that these lessons are given from a place of judgement, but from a place of love.
My father's lesson has been to look at the way he sees perfection.
To understand that it does not exist. We need to look at the examples and situations in life that we are presented with so that we can see this is indeed the case.
My father was presented with two children. Both were born with physical abnormalities. He was married to a wife with emotional challenges. But the key factor affecting my father was his own self judgement and his perception of his own imperfection.
My father had to learn to see the beauty in the different and to accept that each child, no matter how different their life might be and how they may appear to others, that it was these differences that shine out in the light of humanity. That it is important to encourage these children to focus on what they have as a gift and not a curse, and to see that they are not freaks but so very special and are capable of so much in life.

My father needed to see that yes, his life was different, but he was born into this for a reason and that is to teach and show others who have experienced the same, to see things differently.

My mother's lesson is to look at forgiveness. To learn to forgive others, but mostly to forgive herself. When my mother was abused as a child a part of her took it within herself to become the victim, and in some way to feel that she deserved these beatings. Obviously, she did not. My mother's own father was also beaten as a child, and as such the violent pattern continued. My mother still continues to be an angry person. She needs to look within herself to try and forgive others from her past, as to keep this anger, destroys only herself and no one else. My mother wears an inner shield, protecting her from a vulnerability, but to show our vulnerability to others, in the right way, creates empathy, as others see our humanity and humility.

And now my own lessons in life. Self-love.

I was born on St Valentine's day, the day of love, and it is a non-brainer to realize, that in this life time I have had to learn love which has not been easy for me. I have been exposed to situations where self-love has been hard, and my relationship with my mother and in many other situations has been hard. But I feel I have made things difficult myself.

I have always chosen difficult relationships, always looking for someone who is the same as my father so that I can heal them. I know, intuitively that if I do, then I will start the healing process on myself. Achieving a fine line between healing them and providing the place for them to heal is hard but I have never taken the easy pathway, always preferring the difficult one. When I was given an easy marriage I created problems and difficulties, so that I could both suffer and create suffering.

Susanna Dark

When my mother told me that my sister had died that awful time the eight-year-old child that I was smiled and laughed. My mother called me evil and perhaps she was right. I know that I have within me a terrible darkness, I believe that we all have it, but also that we have the choice to use it to harm, or harness it, to see it in its correct context and to use it to heal. It is only through looking at and facing the darkness that we carry within that healing can begin. Running away from it all and burying it only creates even more darkness.
I know that my life's journey is to heal. I am here to be healed and to help and heal others and it is only through self-sacrifice to others that I shall be healed. It is only through self-love and love of others that we can heal.

We are all born into this world as perfect souls. We are full of love, but life in the physical body can be such a painful existence. But, this is the school of life, and as such we have to experience as much as we can. This is the beauty and the pain. We cannot have one without the other. We cannot have the darkness without the light, just as we cannot have the masculine without the feminine.
 It is only through experiencing life that we can grow and become in balance with the beauty we hold inside.
There is a saying, that what is above is also below, and it is also true to say, that what is within is also found without in everyday life.

I'd like to share with you a beautiful technique to use for self-healing, and acceptance called "Ho'Oponopono." This is an Ancient Hawaiian practice of reconciliation and forgiveness.

## Ho'Oponopono

If you're not familiar with the beautiful Heart-healing technique known as Ho'Oponopono, then please try this.

It's the simplest, yet most profound technique I know for opening up your heart and releasing that pent-up emotion.

Right here. Right now.

It's based around four key phrases — perhaps four of the hardest phrases to say. That is why it's so magical. It loosens us up and bring us a new way of thinking and feeling.

Here are the four phrases:

1) I'm sorry.

2) Please forgive me.

3) Thank you.

4) I love you.

I have seen these four phrases used for Ho'Oponopono in every order possible. The way it is listed here is my favourite

Susanna Dark

order, but feel free to say it in a way that feels most authentic and natural for you.

I know that saying that the order is not very important may seem like sacrilege to some, but with Ho'Oponopono as with ANY technique, following your Inner Guidance and making it your own are essential if the technique is to reach your deepest essence. Do what feels right to you.

What I love most about Ho'Oponopono is its simplicity, and how it never gets old. You can do it again and again and still continue to experience new openings of the heart.

At the base of Ho'Oponopono is the concept of total responsibility — not just for your own actions, but for everybody else's too. You are showing up to be a strong, healing presence and will be healed in the process.

This technique has no room for our old self. Connection, clearing and forgiveness are much more important than the concerns of self-pride about who is right and who is wrong. This is a fabulous technique for all forms of healing, healing after an argument, self-healing and healing of others, as all illness comes from a place of self-judgement.

I know it sounds strange but go with it and try it.

So, I had completed my basic research on some illnesses and their causes and everything started to make sense. My readings took on a new form and a new confidence.

## Email Readings

Where as in the past I had conducted Tarot readings via face to face and via the telephone, I found I had a greater confidence to work with email readings. I had a voice to be heard in writing and knew that with an email reading the client would be able to refer to it again and again thereby installing in them, a sense of belief, understanding, and then transformation.

Firstly, I'd like to share with you some information on how I conduct an email reading. I work in the same way as I conduct my face to face readings and telephone readings, using my own intuition and the Tarot and I ask only that the client sends me three questions, or areas that they wish me to focus on.

There is no previous knowledge of the client, no photos, no handwriting.

I totally trust in my gift.

This is an example of an email reading conducted recently for a client. Names have been withheld for client confidentiality.

As you can see from this email reading, the client has emotional issues which have manifested into the physical. I am very direct in the way I deliver my readings. We as readers all work differently. I have been told my clients like it this way and they want to be told it as it is. But, I always work with the utmost love and integrity.

I always start with a general reading first which is firstly to tell the client what I see. Again, my preferred spread to use is the Celtic Cross spread (refer to the last section of the book).

### Email reading for Jo, compiled by Susanna Dark

*"Jo, Lovely to hear from you, and thank you for remembering me after three years.*

*I am so glad that the previous reading helped.*

*I work in exactly the same way as before, nothing has changed accept for the fact that I have gotten older.*

Susanna Dark

*As you know I am a very direct reader, and I shall not hold back but tell you what I see, delivering it with love and integrity.*

*I shall, as before start with a general reading and then move onto the questions or areas specified.*

*Now to the Tarot...*

*When I look at you Jo, I can see someone who wants to aspire to their dreams to be proactive, direct, assertive, but what is crossing this for good or bad is someone who is, at present feeling the exact opposite, grounded, practical, detached from their emotions, resistant to change.*

*When I look to your past I see someone who was very much a free spirit, clever, in fact a very magical creature, and as such you wish to be this way, and to nurture your capabilities.*

*When it comes to your home and relationship life, I see a man where I sense from you a feeling of indecision.*

*When you first met him things were different, perhaps at that time you did not realise the seriousness of the connection, because at that time your head was not in the right place. Your partner entered your life when you were focusing on another priority, and at that time, he was what you needed, but I wonder if you are the person that you were then, and I feel that now your priorities have changed.*

*In the future I continue to see your existing partner in your life, but you would have changed, you will look at making decisions, decisions based on the person you are now, and your needs, not total sacrifice to others, forgetting yourself, concentrating totally on the needs and views of others.*

*Your own mind, and journey will be strong.*

Susanna Dark

*Any upset would have passed, and you will now be able to in your own company, and with another, and be confident and empowered, not feeling guilty that you are being selfish, but enjoy your self time and be able to think.*

*A deep breath will be taken and a sigh of release.*

*This will be a time of some guilt, this will be obvious as you go through this transition of change, but your own sanity, and peace is needed, and you will realise this. You wish to have it, but you are fearful of it too... But change will come, it is inevitable.*

Now to the clients' three questions or areas to focus on.

**1. My health (The client knows that I am not medically trained, but she is asking advice from an intuitive perspective)**

**I have been struggling with a leg pains for the last 3 years which has been difficult to diagnose of what is causing it and what it is. It has been affecting my life greatly. I have seen many doctors, healers, done lots of research. Nothing has helped so far.**

**I recently reduced my work to part time because of that.**

**Can you have some insight into it? Why this is happening also how I can help myself?**

*Well Jo, all illness is psychosomatic which means all is caused by the mind. But not only does our mind create illness, it stops us from being healed, from getting better. Basically, we can only be healed if we really want to be. If we give ourselves permission to be healed. If we feel that we do not deserve it, or that we do not wish to be punished by it. This is what came to me as soon as I read your question, but what I want to do is take a look at you health wise, and then ask the Tarot how you can be healed, what do you need to do medically or other. I think that to visit doctors, healers, and to cut back work is good, but this is only touching the surface and not the root of the problem. The answer lies within you, and I shall now turn to the Tarot, so we can find your answer.*

*Jo as I am writing this I just yawned, its late in the day, and out came the sound of a wolf, the wounded wolf sound. Interesting stuff, and I listen to all the sounds that the universe gives to me.*

*I feel that something that may help you would be a Shamanic Sound Healing, something very similar to the service that they give at the Bridget Healing Centre in Glastonbury.*

*I do not feel that the root of your pain in your leg is muscular but emotional, a deep rooted emotional pain, that needs to be released. I feel that you are holding back the change and transformation that needs to occur in all areas of your life. You need to trust and release. You need to believe in every cell in your body, that this pain no longer belongs to you or your life.*

*This means being brave in changing aspects to your relationship, including the way you perceive it, and also your work.*

*When I look to your past I see someone who was happy, a childlike spontaneous attitude to making choices, to achieving your wishes, and now you wish to aspire to this too.*

*When it comes to work I see self-employment choices for you, and I wonder if you wished to do this in the past but did not follow the idea.*

*But, when I look to the future, there is a great divide, a dividing line between what you wish to do, and what you are actually doing, and then I see someone who is not going with the flow, and stepping into their destiny.*

*You are worried that if you make changes in your life, where will it go? Who can I talk to re this, will it fail?*

*When we have a pain in the leg, it means that our rucksack of life is heavy, that our burdens are too much, that we are unable to stand the frustrations of life, remember the term*

*"I can't stand this much longer".*

*Follow your dreams, act on your hunches, and do not keep yourself small out of fear.*

*Act accordingly. See the shamanic healer, and make changes to your life, and then your leg could get better.*

## 2. Career.

**I have made a decision to go part time because of my pains and feeling that I wish to focus on developing my own businesses. Spiritual Painting, writing, all using my creative talents and other more spiritual abilities.**

**Yet recently I have some doubts if this is the right decision, if I am good enough with my art and how can I help others yet being in pain myself... the calling is strong but not sure why my body is stopping me.**

**My worry is if this is safe for me? Maybe my spiritual development has been causing the pains I have been experiencing? How can I protect myself and in the same time help people?**

*Well I have just answered this in the question above, no your pains are not being caused by doing it, they are being caused by not doing it.*

*Fear causes pain. Step into your power.*

*Well it is funny isn't it Jo, how we can make excuses as to why we can't work at being self-employed, how we* can't make positive changes. We look at the people around us and we believe that they are the reason why we have our limitations.

The negative words that they say, are the words we speak to ourselves.

At present you are holding back, you are the spectator in life rather than the adventurer, and what is causing this is fear.

In the past I can see that you made changes to work, you went with the flow, made decisions based on what others thought, how others acted, you went ahead with the norm, but where was your voice, where did you shine?

Now you are aware of your partner, and his thoughts and ideas, but part of you feels that he could be holding you back, but he is not holding you back, in fact no one is, well one person is, and this is you!

You are holding yourself back.

In the future I see a situation where you will look at what is right for you. Where you will stand in your own power, from a perspective of empowerment, where you will make the right choices based on the now.

What will come will be a catalyst, where great change will come to your life, this catalyst will be an argument, a conflict, but this will be followed by a sense of extreme peace, and a contract or legality which will change your working life, at the time you will be worried, without a sense of strength or determination, but you will need to trust, and know that spirit is with you at this time.

Understand that sometimes we need to be brave in life, we need to just take that step into the unknown, without a safety blanket, and know that if we do, with love in our hearts, that we shall be fine.

Susanna Dark

*In answer to your specific questions, your body is not holding you back, it is fear that is holding you back.*

*You fear is creating the pains, not the spiritual work you are doing, but if you are fearful that during practice you might be taking on others pain, then look at guarding yourself.*

*Learn some techniques to shield yourself during work, and when you initially ground out, ask your guides to protect you.*

*This will come with time and practice, but it will come.*

*I shall not answer any more questions on this. I have only one thing to say. Jo, just do it.*

*Stop making excuses, and just do it.*

*Spirit is giving you a kick up the backside.*

*This is your time, and if you hide behind others, then you are not walking your truth. I shall say no more.*

## 3. Relationship.

**I have been in a relationship for the last 5 years. My condition created some difficulties between us. I am a bit lost with my current feelings and his feelings towards me. We are trying our best but the conflicts are quite often between us. Any light in this?**

*I shall take a look at the dynamics behind the relationship, the future, and then take a look at your partner.*

*Just as I am dealing the cards, spirit tells me that you must find your own voice. I can see that subconsciously you are carrying some upset within, and that is due to negativity. In the past, in this relationship you have felt very much like the spectator, and that has been due to fear.*

*You feel that others are holding you back, others that comment on your working life, also comment on your relationship, and instead of listening to your own inner voice, you have held back and listened to them, and the opinions that they have.*

*Stop this, and listen to yourself, speaking from a place of truth, not fear!*

*In the future I see you still with your current partner, where his ideas and direction do strive to move you forwards, but, due to your positive thought process you will run with him, rather than against him.*

*The major factor that will bring forth this change will be your change in work.*

*Once you find your happiness then you find that everything else falls into place.*

*The pain in your leg is due to you holding yourself back, and not listening to your inner voice due to unnecessary fear.*

*Now to your partner I wish to look at him, and then how he sees you, and then to the questions that you have specified.*

*When I look at your partner I sense a feeling of imbalance and what is causing this is his current work, or new work.*

*In the past he has been wearing the mask of bravado, pretending that all has been ok, but in fact he has not been knowing himself, or what he has been wanting.*

*Now he feels guilty for being this way, acting this way, in the past.*

*I feel that both of you are stuck, and both need to make life choices, and changes in your life.*

*The term the blind leading the blind comes to mind, and yes, I can see the frustration and conflict that you have in the relationship, but this is normal to a degree.*

*I can see that he, in some part wants the relationship to end, but he fears this too, because predominantly he cares for you.*

*He sees you for the person that you are, but can see that you are stuck, with your emotions, and thoughts, but he remembers a time in his past when he was this way too.*

*In the future I see your partner feeling more empowered work wise, with choices that he will make, that will make him happier.*

*When he thinks about you he wants to be with you and nurture this relationship but he feels that he cannot communicate.*

*In the past he can see how you have battled with your emotions and carried unhappiness within, he can see how you are wanting to be proactive with your life, and how frustrating it is for you.*

*He loves you for the person that you are.*

*The fact that you are real, you are genuine, warts and all, and he likes the fact that there is no pretence.*

*All the things that you see as being a challenge, and where you judge yourself, he understands and takes these as being part of you.*

*In the future I still see the love being there, he just worries about your working life, and the fact that you worry that you are slow.*

*He sees you as a magical person, he feels comfortable with you, and has focus on the future.*

Susanna Dark

*Jo moving to your question, yes you are both lost, but I do not feel that it is all to do with your relationship.*

*I feel that outside factors, like work, lifestyle and emotions are to do with this. It is normal. All relationships go through their ups and downs.*

*The most important thing is that you love each other, from a root perspective.*

*In the next eight months all will change. Your magic will shine through and you will know where you are going in life, with your work and relationship.*

*Conflicts have their purpose, it is a release mechanism, but I do believe that is because you need to embrace change, and one of you is very resistant, due to fear, to embrace this. You must embrace this, because change is inevitable, if you do not, then a catalyst comes, and breaks it up, as the water cannot keep being blocked, things crack eventually.*

*Jo if you take anything from this reading today it is to embrace change. Take that step, take that risk, and embrace it with love. You are not alone, I am fighting for your corner.*

*Much love, Sue"*

# CHAPTER 7

## Moving On and a Time for Expansion

In 2010 we moved to Cornwall and in 2011 I opened my own shop Wise Old Crow in Bude. It was a tiny little unit in an Arcade in The Strand Shopping Centre. The shopping centre was run down with hardly any of the units occupied. This was the time of another financial recession, but I had been led to the centre by my own intuition, so I needed to take that risk.

I decorated my shop with posters of Tarot cards such as The Empress, The High Priestess and The Death Card, and I chose images from The Rider Waite Tarot deck created by the artist Pamela Colman Smith. Later, out of sheer coincidence, I found out that Pamela had in fact spent her latter years in Bude.

I sold new age items in my shop and conducted readings, but this little unit was far from perfect where the readings were concerned. The client and I had no privacy, and every time I conducted a reading I had to lock the shop door.

Then back in 2013 I decided to expand. I had found out some useful information about one of the largest units in the centre that had previously been a number of different outlets, but each had not worked for the owner. The largest unit had a separate room out the back that had been used as a store room. This would be ideal as a reading room, a place to conduct my readings in private. I immediately contacted the landlord and pledged my claim to the shop.

For a few years I ran my shop as a place of selling goods and conducting readings, but then in 2016 the dynamics of the business changed. I started to hold talks and I invited authors to conduct book signings. I started to run groups on intuitive Tarot reading and psychic development. With regards to the intuitive Tarot group, whereas previously I had been teaching this method on a one to one basis, I now had a group of nine woman who had an interest in the Tarot and who owned their own deck. (And yes, some had stored it away in their set of drawers, never to see the light of day again!) Now I could offer them the opportunity to study the Tarot and connect to it intuitively. They also craved a new way of learning and they also wished to form their own meanings and connect deeper to achieve transformation.

Initially, when we first started together and after journeying with each card, their findings were brief. Very much like the accompanying paper booklet you get with a deck. But once they gained confidence and became more relaxed, trusting the system and the messages they received from their inner voice, they started to produce valid messages for themselves that made perfect sense.

We also implemented practice readings in the sessions where participants read for themselves and each other.

To begin with they could only do readings from their own deck of Tarot cards, but then after a while they became confident enough to read from any deck. The Tarot began talking intuitively to them at all times.

As I am writing this, we have two more cards to journey with and then our journey will be complete.

We have also booked our local hall for an afternoon to hold a charity Tarot reading event. The group really wanted a way to practice and show how they have grown throughout the process.

Susanna Dark

Yesterday I held a new one-day workshop which I have created for a group of lovely people on intuitive Tarot reading, with one lady participant commenting on how "simple it all was".

And me, well I continue conducting readings for my clients, using not just the Tarot, but my natural intuition and bit of intuitive astrology too. I'm also able at times to connect mediumistic-ally, bringing through the spirits of our departed loved ones.

I always use knowledge gained on my journey and the most important thing I impart to my clients during a reading is to find their own empowerment and own happiness.

My clients often say to me "Thanks Sue, this reading has been really helpful. You really are a Life Saver"

A Tarot life saver...perhaps?

Susanna Dark

## The Fools (Intuitive) Journey. (My version)

Now for a story within a story. As I have already said, the Tarot is really a narrative of a soul's journey through life. This is my version of the story and all the actors that play the parts are all the cards in The Major Arcana.

Welcome the players. The scene is set by using "The Tarot Of The Old Path" For those of you using a custom set e.g "The Rider Waite Tarot", I have included the standard names.

0. The Fool
1. The Magician
2. The High Priestess
3. The Empress
4. The Emperor
5. The High Priest
6. The Lovers
7. Mastery (The Chariot)
8. Strength
9. The Wise One (The Hermit)
10. The Wheel Of Fortune
11. Justice
12. The Lone Man (The Hanged Man)
13. The Close (Death)
14. The Guide (Temperance)
15. Temptation ( The Devil)
16. The Tower
17. The Star
18. Ilusion (The Moon)
19. The Sun
20. Karma (Judgement)
21. The World

This is a story, a fool's story, of life and intuition and as with all good stories it begins with….

Once upon a time The Fool (0) went on a walk. This Fool was embarking on a new journey, he was brave and focussed. He was on a mission. His mission was an adventure. He had places to see and people to meet. He had been planning this for a long time.

As he proceeded on his journey he came across a strange looking fellow in an area of open woodland. This man was dressed in a cloak, and in his hand he held a Wand. This was The Magician (1) Surrounding The Magician were tools of his Craft, A Chalice, An Athame, and A Pentacle.

"Why hello," The Magician said, "Where are you going dear Fool"

The Fool replied, "I am off on an adventure!"

"Well then", The Magician replied, "you may take with you my tools of life. They may just come in handy. You see, life gives you all the tools that you need, you just have to find them and know how to use them," The Fool thanked The Magician and continued on his way.

Next appeared a creature of beauty and wisdom. The Fool had encountered The High Priestess (2). "Who are you?" The Fool asked. "I am the High Priestess" she replied, "I stand in between the two pillars of darkness and light. I achieve balance in life and as such I am in a position to give you advise on your journey. Always listen to your intuition for it is a valuable tool that many ignore. It will be your greatest guide and tell you what choices to make. Try not to just listen to others, but look within, for your own answers."

The Fool took The High Priestess' advice on board, and as he departed thanked her for her insight.

Walking further on, The Fool met The Empress (3). She was sitting on a rock, heavily pregnant, with another small child on her lap. The Fool did not initially want to disturb her, but he knew that she was part of his journey, so as such, he approached her.

"Greetings Fool, you are on a very exciting journey of new beginnings" The Empress said. "I, as The Empress, represent fertility, abundance and self-empowerment. The gift I give you is of self-nurturing. This will be a lonely journey for you at times, so to be able to find solace in your own company is important, but equally important is to know that you are never truly alone." "Thank you" replied The Fool.

Next to greet The Fool was the The Emperor (4). "I am here today to teach you wisdom, for yourself and others" imparted The Emperor. "It is fine to be able to passionately embrace your new journey with excitement, but I want to impart to you my knowledge and practicality. My advice to you today is not to act in impulse. This can create issues, and you could make the wrong choice. Think before you act, take a deep breath, and think slowly and logically. Never let your heart dominate your mind. I impart this wisdom to you today."

Next to feature in The Fools journey was The High Priest (5). He sat on a throne surrounded with religious objects. His right hand was raised in blessing, and it reminded the Fool of the time when he went to church and received a blessing. The High Priest said. "I am here to bless your journey. May god be with you. Remember that you have your spirituality. Your own religion. May your journey be a spiritual pilgrimage, and may you find your own god."

The Fool was slightly confused and overwhelmed by now. So much advice in such a short time. This journey was going to be very interesting, and he hoped that he had not bitten off more than he could chew, but he continued walking on his journey.

Next, amongst a clearing the fool came across The Lovers (6). A naked man and a woman seated together and absolutely unaware of anyone else around them. They showed by their togetherness a love for themselves and all of nature. The Fool felt embarrassed and did not know where to look and wondered why they were naked in such a public place. "I suppose you are wondering why we are naked," the couple said. "Well I didn't like to ask!" the Fool thought to himself! "We are naked because we have nothing to hide. We are naked in truth and ask that you follow your own inner truth on this journey. If you speak your truth to yourself and others, then nothing can go wrong"

The Fool thanked the couple but decided not to stay any longer in their presence, he did not need any distractions from his journey, so he walked on. The Fool should have been looking where he was going, but The Lovers had been more of a distraction then he realised. As a result, The Fool nearly got knocked over by an approaching chariot. "Hey hold on!", he shouted. "You nearly ran me over!" Mastery (7) replied "Your imagination has been occupying you, looking at The Lovers. If you look closely at me you can see that I am not moving. My horses are undecided. In fact, I am undecided as to where I am going. I am so pleased that you have planned your journey and you know where you are going. I have so much power in my hands with these horses, but I do not know what to do with it. My advice to you, dear Fool is to take one step at a time. I have too many horses on this chariot, and as such I am confused. Take one step and enjoy each one that you take. Life is a journey and should be enjoyed, making as many memories as possible rather than rushing through it.

The Fool uttered his thanks and good byes and continued on his journey, but by now his rucksack was getting heavy and he needed a break. Sitting by a glorious red, orange and brown rug he took a rest. This is not a rug he realised, the rug was making growling noises, and much to his horror and fear he realised he was sitting next to a Lion. "I am Strength" (8) the Lion said. "I represent strength for you but also for others. When you stroke my mane, not only does it make you feel calm, but it calms me too, and this is the gift that I give you today, the gift of strength through adversity. When you are feeling irritated on your journey or troubled, know that you are in fact stronger than you appear. Just look within and reflect on the fact that you have already completed much of your journey already. This is an accomplishment to be proud of for it shows your inner strength." The Fool waved good bye, thanking the lion for his advice. He was then met by the next character on his journey, The Wise One (9).

"I am the Wise One, I am here to talk to you about what you have achieved so far on your journey, but no only that, with my lantern I shall light your way forwards. I am old. I have had many of my own journeys, but my message to you today is that you ask for guidance from those that you would not usually ask. You are a young man and do not have much life experience. I am asking that you not to have any fear when it comes to talking to others. Just because a man looks old does not mean that they are incapacitated or incapable. Talk to as many people as you can and learn from their stories and memories.

"Thank you," The Fool replied, "I will try and be humble".

"The next card you shall encounter shall not be a person but an object. This object is an item of desire, The Wheel of Fortune" (10) the Wise One added.

And as The Fool continued on with his journey he saw to his right a beautiful bright wheel. Around this wheel's circumference he saw people dressed in beautiful attire, and within the wheel were the seasons of life.

"I wonder what this means?" The Fool thought.

"I am the tale of life. I am that which comes around, then goes around", replied The wheel. "I talk about the simple celebration of life, and that to achieve happiness is to understand that life really is simply a celebration. You as humans make it complicated, and every time you complicate matters something goes wrong and then the wheel of life has to turn again. The wheel continues to turn until you learn that life need not be complicated, need not be stressful and challenging. The wheel is symbolic of the world and mother earth, and if we respect her and the seasons we shall live our lives in harmony".

"Thank you, that makes total sense," said The Fool. "I shall remember this." And then off he went, maybe a little too fast, as he bumped right into Justice (11) wearing his long ornate robe with the set of scales in his hand. "Are you not sorry that you did not stay longer with that Wheel of Fortune" said Justice. "Life is very serious you know. All of this rushing around from one card to another. Do you really feel that you will get any true benefit from your adventure? I am the card of balance, equilibrium and righteousness. I demand that before you leave me today, you take stock in what you have learned so far on your journey, so that you may continue with a clear conscience, ready to proceed. For if you are not accountable for your actions and thoughts, how can you make room in your mind for more ideas to come and for more adventures. You need to close one door before you open another one, surely?"

The Fool slowly tiptoed away from The Justice card, he was putting a huge dampener on his journey, and The Fool really wanted to be enjoying it. "There has already been so much advise and so much to learn," he thought." So much seriousness and intensity, surely my adventure should be fun?" he thought, and just as he thought this he saw something that made him laugh out loud, a court jester in full dress hanging upside down from a tree.

"I love to hang upside down", The Lone Man (12) said. "It helps me see things from totally a different perspective. You know sometimes when you are stuck and you just can't see out of a situation? Seeing it from a different perspective just seems to help. I have perfected this so beautifully that I can hang on one leg. I love it!"

The Fool decided that the best way to go along with this was to try it himself, and yes, by hanging upside down the world did look very different indeed. It made him feel a bit sick and topsy-turvy, but hey what an experience! As The Fool returned back to his normal position, he vowed to start seeing things differently. It could be fun, and maybe he would eventually be able to balance on one leg!

Continuing on with his journey, The Fool noticed that the clouds were becoming darker. Night time was coming. He had not noticed the time, so decided to take shelter under a tree. His rucksack would make a good pillow under his head, and as he nodded off into the land of sleep he started to dream. The dream of the dead. In this dream a Grim Reaper was standing betwixt an owl and a baby. "Who are you" the Fool asked. "I am The Close" (13) the figure replied. "Does this mean that I am not going to be able to finish my journey?", The Fool asked. "No." said The Close. "I am symbolic of death and rebirth, of endings and new beginnings. I clear away the old and take away the dead. For how can new babies come into a world that is full of the old? Change is essential to make way for the new. If change does not occur then imbalance takes place, and sickness, misery and hardship dominate. It is the law of the universe. To bring in the new, the old must pass." The Fool felt a tear roll down his cheek. He knew about death as his grandfather had recently passed over. But he learned today about how important change was. Change that was feared by many. Change that was so very essential.

"Why do people fear change, Grim Reaper?" The Fool asked. "Because they become set in their ways" he replied. "They get used to even the dysfunctional, becoming lazy and complacent. When they become stagnant they then become fearful, fearful of the new."

"I will try and embrace change", The Fool replied. The dream then started to fade and The Fool realised that the dream he had experienced was a powerful dream, perhaps brought to him as a spiritual message from The Guide (14) a guide that was with him for this journey. This guide was a protector, and if he listened to this inner guide, then it would protect him from any Fear (15) that he may have during this journey. The fool realised that in order to achieve his dreams and wishes, (16), that fear was part of the process, that he needed to see the darkness before the light, and that any fear he may experience was simply Illusion (17).

By now day light had come, and the day was turning out to be beautiful. The Sun (18) was shining, and The Fool, hopped, jumped and skipped full of the joy of life and the moment itself. He felt young and totally connected to his inner child within. Suddenly this journey made sense. He had an inner sense of belonging and knowing (19). He knew exactly who he was and where he was going. Everything in life felt connected and he felt a sense of inner peace (20). He now realised that the journey he was taking was not to a destination, but was there for a reason, and that each character that he encountered was a symbolic part of the journey, a journey of discovery, to himself. (21)

The End.

# AFTERWORD

We as humans have the ability to heal. Not only others but ourselves. We are beautiful beings of love that can create miracles.
But, most of us have forgotten this unless we are working with understanding ourselves and others. We can become slaves to a society where we are chained to our ego and to the material things in life.
We need to listen to our own inner voice of truth, not isolate ourselves into a system where what you have, and who you are, shouts louder than, "I care about you, and I love you and myself unconditionally."
Some of us judge ourselves based on our own unrealistic perception of life and how we think we should be. We feel that we are the measure of our own imperfections, rather than focusing on what we really are and building on these unique and beautiful qualities. This brings forth a lack of self-love.
Some are just takers, taking from one another, taking from Mother Earth and giving nothing back, raping the earth, and as such have created such an imbalance. Humanity is sick. It is a sickness of the mind, body and soul.
Some no longer care what they do, what they eat, or what they say.
Only when we all wake up and take responsibility for ourselves, our lives and the planet, will things change. Only when we all start to give back to the Earth, when we start to listen, in meditation and in prayer, will we remember that we are part of a collective, not separate from each other.
It is so very easy to blame illness, and our lives on others, but we are the creators, the manifestation of all. This is not from a self-judgment perspective, but from a self-awareness

perspective. When we take charge of our lives then change can occur for all.

We must give ourselves permission, without judgment to bring forth this change.

All healing comes from a place of love. Love of ourselves and others.

Really, all we need is love.

Brightest Blessings x

# APPENDIX

### Further Exercises and ideas

Here are some further exercises and ideas to work with to heighten your intuitive powers and become more adept at reading the Tarot.

### How to choose a Tarot deck – Intuitively

As mentioned earlier, by tradition you are supposed to have a Tarot deck chosen for you, as a gift by another, but I personally do not believe this. It is important that you choose your own deck.

There are so many tarot decks available on the market from The Egyptian Tarot, to Tarot of the Cats, To The Witches Tarot, the traditional Rider Waite Tarot, The Gummy Bears Tarot.... (yes, I know, crazy eh?) and in a New Age shop, confronted by all these decks it is so easy to become overwhelmed.

The two traditional Tarot decks that I usually recommend are either The Rider Waite Tarot deck or The Morgan Greer Tarot. That is because the imagery is easy on the eye, and they are both brilliant as starter decks for the novice. I have though, known of many advanced Tarot readers that have stuck with the Rider Waite all their lives after forming a good relationship with the deck itself.

When selecting your deck take a look at either the imagery on the back of the packaging, or if this is not possible (not all decks show the cards in the pack on the back) then research by looking at the internet. Look at the imagery and see if it is talking to you. I get a lot of customers who will purchase a deck based on their own pathway that they are following, or their personal likes. Someone will purchase a mermaid Tarot deck because they love mermaids. Another, Tarot of the Cats, you get where I am coming from here. But to be able to purchase a Tarot deck because it is speaking to you intuitively is often the key to finding one exactly right for you.

When looking at the imagery either by looking on the internet, or on the back of the packaging of the deck, still your mind, and then look at each image at a time, and see if a story is unwinding in your mind. If this is not the case, then see if trigger words are coming to you. Maybe the deck is making you feel a certain way, releasing an emotion. Perhaps the imagery could be bringing up memories from your past. This is telling you that you are connecting to the deck, and that this is the one you need to work with. Not only as a divination tool, but this deck may be the one to help you find out more about yourself, bringing in the new, making new discoveries, and unlocking new doors to self-discovery.

I shall warn you though that becoming a Tarot collector is an easy addiction to have. Once a Tarot deck starts to talk to you, you rapidly find that more do too. Each Tarot deck has a story to tell, with different imagery and ways of expressing the story through this imagery. It is fun, and I myself have been a collector for years though I have recently slimmed down my collection. Just, please if we meet, do not tell me you have "The gummy bears Tarot"!

Susanna Dark

## Colours and the Tarot.

I love working with colours. Have you noticed how we react to colours every day of our lives, from a grey miserable rainy day to a bright sunny day?

Colours instantly affect us. Just by putting on a new red jacket, to a green scarf or a black skirt can affect us. The red makes us feel alive, passionate and responsive. The green, natural, healthy and aware, and black, passionate, mysterious, and secretive.

One of the easiest ways to work intuitively with the Tarot is via colour.

Go through your Tarot deck, perhaps start from The Major Arcana and choose a card colour-wise that represents a place where you want to be.

If you want to have some passion in your life, find a card with red as a predominant colour, and place this Tarot card in a place where you can see it during the day, for example by your bed or in the kitchen area. Your subconscious mind will soon take it in, and as such your mood will adjust accordingly.

For a more intensive effect, meditate on this card, as per the intuitive Tarot meditation, and find out what this colour is trying to say to you.

What message is that card wanting to bring to your life? Find out how this card can help you release an emotional blockage.

## The Elements, Intuitive Astrology and the Tarot.

I wanted to add an extra element to this book, for those of you that have been working through the exercises and have found your confidence and want to look further at connecting intuitively in alternative ways.

I wanted to look at the Elements and Intuitive Astrology within the Tarot itself.

We as humans are made up chemically of four elements, earth, air, fire and water.

Our body is made of what we eat, vegetation grown from the earth, our lungs are full of the air that we breath, and we drink the water that makes up a large proportion of our bodies. Fire is the passion we contain within. Our essence the blood that flows through our veins.

Sometimes though, it almost appears that we can be, from an intuitive perspective, more of one element than another.

If you perceive the elements from an intuitive astrological perspective, you will see that the Air signs, Aquarius, Gemini, and Libra, are the dreamers, the ideas people, chatty and at time air heads.

The Earth signs are the Taureans, the Virgos, and the Capricorns. These are the steadfast grounded signs, the reliable people, that get things done. The givers, but also the stubborn ones.

The Fire signs are the Leos, the Sagittarians, and The Arians. These are the charismatic characters. The smooth talkers, but also the vibrant, dynamic workaholics, with generous natures.

Lastly, we have the Water signs, the Cancerians, the Pisceans and the Scorpios, the sensitive bunch, able to mould themselves around people. These are the natural intuitives, but also the carers.

Have you ever chatted to someone and had a feeling that they were a particular astrological sun sign? Did they seem like an air head to you, or stuck in their ways, stubborn? Were they over emotional, dramatic?

Did you intuitively feel that they were a particular sun sign? Well then, they had an element that was dominant within them.

Perhaps they were a Scorpio, a water sign, and as such were over emotional and wore their hearts on their sleeve. They looked for drama in life, to be able to express their emotions, to enable them to communicate with others and to feel a sense of connectedness.

Were they detached emotionally, practical and matter of fact? Were they steadfast and reliable, always wanting to help? Did they loved being outdoors connecting with nature? Well then, they were an Earth sign, most probably a Taurean.

Another example, are they a bit scatter brained, are they wacky, forward thinkers, and trend setters? If they appeared detached emotionally and enjoyed their own company then they were most likely an Aquarian.

Working with the elements and astrology from an intuitive perspective is just another way of connecting to the Tarot, understanding yourself, and the person you are reading for.

Below are the elements, and the cards that I feel are relevant to that element. When you journey with the cards yourself, you will see all the attributes of each card, its element and it will speak for itself.

I have chosen two cards for each element, one from The Major Arcana and the other Minor Arcana. Again, I am using The Tarot of the Old Path.

**Earth** - strength, the ability to stand firm, solidity, thinking deeply, inner strength, attunement with the rhythm of the biological life.

Corresponding cards - The Wise One and The King Of Pentacles

**Water** - The womb of biological life, the memory of evolution, being nourished by past experience, floating in the now and not being afraid where it will take you. Nurturing yourself and others.

Corresponding cards – The Empress and The Queen Of Cups.

**Air** - The rhythm of breath with the planet. The ability to change, the ability to make changes. The ability to accept those things which have changed. The ability to just fly when you need to. Independence. Acknowledging that you cannot teach without learning. The smallest movements can lead to the largest of effects.

Corresponding cards – The High Priestess and The Ace of Swords.

**Fire** - Accepting an initiating change, clearing away the old and making space for the new, cleansing and rejuvenating.

Corresponding cards – The Fool and The Ace of wands.

Again, make sure that you listen to your inner voice of intuition whilst using the elements.

If you feel that whilst searching for a Tarot card to represent the element you see within the imagery a more relevant card than the one I have listed here, if it's talking to you, then make sure you use it, as this is the key to your inner magick.

### Relaxation technique to eliminate stress in the body

This exercise is called, Progressive muscle relaxation.

Many of us live in a chronic state of muscular tension. It gets worse when we face times of increased stress. You've already learned that whenever you experience anxiety it's expressed in your body. You may not even realize that your muscles are tense all the time.

Think about what you do when you're stressed. Do you tense your shoulders, frown, clench your jaw, or hold your breath?

For this exercise, you're going to purposely tense your muscles and then relax them. This will allow you to learn to recognize when your muscles are tense and when they are relaxed. Becoming mindfully aware of the difference between tension and relaxation creates an internal physical alarm, which will let you know when you're starting to feel stressed so that you can do something about it.

For this exercise, please find a quiet place, free of distractions. You may choose to lie down with a pillow under your knees or sit in a chair.

As you work through this exercise, you'll squeeze different muscles as hard as you can, making sure not to squeeze them too hard, or so long, that it causes you any harm. You'll tighten the different muscles enough to create discomfort so that you can begin to learn about how your body experiences and expresses stress and pain. Then you will rapidly release the tension all at once.

- Take two deep breaths. Make sure your breathing is slow, smooth, even, quiet and long. Breathe in from your toes to the top of your head and exhale from your head down through to your toes. This is one complete breath. First, you'll feel the resting sensations in your body as you complete these first two breath-cycles. You'll initially focus on becoming aware of what's going on in your body.

- Start with your forehead. *Lift your eyebrows* as high as they can go. Lift them to the top of your head! Focus on the feeling in the muscle with this intense contraction. If there's a lot of pain, then just ease off a bit. Breathe in slowly, deeply and quietly. Hold the squeeze for as long as it takes to slowly breathe in. Don't hold your breath. When you're ready to breathe out, quickly release the tensed muscle. Just let it go. Allow the muscle to completely relax as you exhale slowly and deeply. Notice how different that muscle feels when it's tense compared to when it's relaxed.

- Move to your eyes. *Squeeze your eyes tightly shut*. Hold the squeeze for a breath-cycle and then relax. Breathe deeply for two more breath-cycles and feel the relaxed sensation in your eyes.

- Move on to your mouth. *Open your mouth* as wide as you can. Hold your jaw as wide open as you can. Squeeze as long as you breathe in and then let go quickly as you breathe out. Don't force your breath out, just let it release naturally and smoothly.

- Next *lift your shoulders* to your ears. Tense them and then relax. Imagine your breath going into your shoulders and releasing any remaining tension. Notice how your shoulders feel when they're tight compared to when you let go of that tension. Focus on the relaxation in your shoulders for two more breaths.

- Bring both of *your arms up to your shoulders and clench your fists*. Tighten both your arms as much as you can. Feel that tension. Only tense your arms and fists. Don't clench your jaw or raise your shoulders. Breathe in and tighten and then drop your arms. Breathe deeply into both your arms for two breath-cycles. When doing these exercises try not to tense any other parts of your body except for the specific muscle group you're working with. Just imagine your breath going into your arm muscles and back out. Relax them even more as you breathe out. Breathe in and focus on your arms and breathe out and relax.

- Next make a tight *fist with both of your hands* at the same time. Tighten them. Tighter. Tighter… and breathe out and release the fists. Focus on how your hands feel afterward. Breathe in and out for two more breaths.

- Take a deep breath and *expand your chest a*s wide as it will go. Notice the feeling of tightness in your chest. Then quickly release the tension in the chest as you breathe out. Breathe deeply, gently and smoothly letting your stomach expand as you breathe in. Focus on the sensation in your chest as you breathe for two more breaths.

- • Bring your attention to your abdomen and *squeeze your belly button* so that it tries to touch your spine. Keep squeezing for as long as you can as you take a slow, deep inhalation. At the end of the inhalation let all the tension go quickly and then continue to breathe into your abdomen for two more slow deep breaths.

- *Tighten the muscles in your buttocks*. Hold that tension as you breathe in and let go of the tension all at once as you breathe out. Just rest and breathe feeling the sensation of relaxation in those muscles. Breathe for two more complete breaths as you bring your attention to your buttocks.

- *Flex both of your feet* by stretching your feet upward toward your shins. You're just tensing up your feet and your leg muscles here. Feel the tension in your thighs and lower legs. Hold the tension. Tense up both your legs. Notice how that tension feels and then let it all go. Breathe for two more complete breaths as you feel the physical sensation of release in your feet and thighs.

- Finally, *curl your toes*. Really tighten them up as you breathe in. Curl those toes tightly and release them as you breathe out. Bring your attention to the feeling in your toes for two more complete breaths.

- At the end of the exercise, when you're ready, open your eyes. Start to move your body, slowly at first. Again, if you're doing this exercise on the floor, roll onto your right side first; push yourself up to a sitting position with your arms. Stand up very slowly.

## Ways to develop your intuition

Quiet your mind and listen. Take time each day to experience silence. Practice calming your mind by using whatever breathing or meditative technique you prefer. Let go of the inclination to think, or analyse, and trying to know everything. Be open and listen. Let your thoughts roam and be open to the ideas and solutions that come to you. When you listen to your intuition it connects you with a greater knowledge. It usually communicates through symbols, feelings and emotions.

Learn to trust your hunches and gut feelings. If something doesn't feel right the chances are it isn't. What may be right for one person could be totally wrong for you. How many times have you had that feeling in your stomach compelling you to do, or not do, something for no apparent reason? Listening to it probably helped you avoid a traffic accident or led you to be at the right place and time for getting that great job or meeting that special person. Your intuition is your inner guide, so learn to trust it. At first, trusting it may be a bit scary, but allow it the opportunity to develop.

Pay attention and be aware. In order to increase your intuitive abilities, you must pay attention to what is going on around you. The more data and information you absorb from your environment, the more your subconscious mind has to work with when you have to make an important decision. Since your intuition uses the information gathered by the conscious mind, the more you have available, the better the solution.

Remember, the subconscious mind communicates information to the conscious mind through your intuition.

Other types of intuition reveal themselves in thought flashes or inspiration. The key is to take notice. The more you pay attention, the more of them you will experience. If you've ever ignored your intuition and then had to deal with unpleasant ensuing circumstances, you know what it feels like. To prevent such mishaps, make sure to pay attention to the tiny hints and clues you receive.

Employ your subconscious while you sleep.

Before you go to bed at night, reflect upon questions and issues for which you couldn't find solutions during the day. Think about and explore different possibilities. This will trigger your imagination and put your subconscious to work at furnishing you with creative solutions while you sleep. Be sure to have a pen and paper handy, so when you wake up during the night with some great ideas, you can write them down in a journal.

 When you take time to write your journal, you tap into thoughts, feelings and ideas you're not typically conscious of. This is an excellent way to release inner messages, insights or hidden knowledge about a situation or problem that requires attention.

The Benefits of Developing Your Intuition

- Helps you reduce stress by identifying and dealing with problems more effectively
- Unleashes your creativity and imagination
- Puts you in touch with your subconscious, and therefore helps you uncover hidden truths about yourself and situations in your life
- By being in touch with your intuition, you prevent the build-up of negative emotions and thinking
- Integrates left and right brain functions giving you a more complete perspective on issues
- Helps you make better, more integrative decisions
- Improves physical, mental and emotional health.

Developing your intuition is like learning any new skill. The more you practice, the better you get at it. As with any new exercise or routine you're not used to, start off slowly and gradually build your "intuitive muscles."

## Creative writing using the Tarot

For a quick half hour exercise, why not try writing an essay using a Tarot card. What can be more inspiring than gazing in day dream at The Lovers card from The Major Arcana and writing a wonderfully romantic story or poem based on this card.

It reminds me of the tale of "Romeo and Juliet" by Shakespeare.

To shake the story up a bit, why not create your own version of this famous play and use other Tarot cards to create new characters. These can be from the Minor Arcana. You could change the ending, and instead of making it a dramatic tale of love and death, give it a happy ending by incorporating The Sun and The Chariot Card from The Major Arcana, "…and Romeo and Juliet journeyed into the sun set and lived happily ever after".... Sounds fab, or too good to be true? The choice, or course, is yours.

## Writing Poetry using the Tarot

I found a few beautiful Tarot poems on line, but I am sure you can do better.

### "Fool" (Author unknown)

You start your journey, the moment the world became your cradle
Experience the possibilities of many opportunities
The cards have yet to determine your precise future
Can't you hear the chuckling of amusement?

Your bonds will create an sense of connection
The strings tangle when dealt with confusion
Are you able to turn zero into one
The dog following close behind whispering when you might fall

"Your dreams move you forward."

### "Tarot "(Author unknown)

The devil
He's the first card drawn
Evil grin with servants serving him
They could break free of their chains

Only held by mentality
Time to break free
Of this reality.

Next the star
But, look at that
I guess I'll be reading it upside down
Flipped on its head that is what it said
Spiritually speaking you're confused
You don't know the rules
Of the game you're playing
So you just lost hope
Day to day seems mundane
Everything is always the same
Dwelling on the negative
Ignoring the positive
The star is saying
Just open your eyes.

Oh hello, Mr. Magician
I see you've joined the gang
You've come to tell me about my day to day
Lost touch of reality
Feet aren't on the ground
Tell me Mr. Magic man, how can I get down?
You're confused and you're lonely
Just listen to The Star
Open your eyes and see who you are.

Now it is explained, Mr. Magic
Now as I'm wielding this three of swords
Rejection and loss
Things ever present in your life
And to fill your future with strife
So this is a warning
Please beware
That danger is lurking
So tread with care

But, do not shy away, I say
Learn to live and love the day to day pain
Keep in touch with it
Before the sun comes the rain.

A young man is next
The Page of Cups

I'm sorry for your bad luck
For it is flipped on its side
Check your addictions
You might want to have a look
Don't let this person hurt you
Whether it be you or another
Insecure and abusive
Don't give him too much
For he wants much and gives none
Just seek who it is
We're just about done.

What a fitting end
The last card reads "Death"
Lucky for you
The meaning is reversed
With that being said
Please don't think you're cursed
This means transformation, a rebirth
Major change is near and dear
So please, do not fear
Let go of the past
Let it linger no longer
Let go of your hurt
Fill it with desire
Accept the change that is beside you
And no longer will you feel like you're stuck.

I hope I have helped
With this reading I've prepared

Susanna Dark

Each card holding relevance
Don't believe?
Turn the other cheek, if you dare.


### "The Magician" (Nicholas Stiltner)

Upon reading my cards of tarot,
(The ones the mystics use,
The cards that unveil the mystery of next)
I gasped, and my throat became narrow
For I'd received reaffirmation of my quest.

The question posed, the riddle pressed,
"Should I continue this scribble, to speak my written word?
With countless doubts my head be vexed!"
But upon drawing, my mind broke free of this malevolent hex.

My pulse quickened and my hands shook
For I saw what even the greats needed to see.
The card that lay softly in my palm
Be that of The Magician, donning his crown of Infinity.


(Poem inspired by the Major Arcana Card "Judgment")

### "Time Of The End" (Unknown)

There comes a time in your life

When you look at where you're gone

And the child within you wonders what went wrong:

All your dreams have turned to dust,

Susanna Dark

You hear strangers in your mind,

And the days go by like friends you left behind -

But when all is said and done

You're not the only one

And you realise that life has just begun.

First you're sorry, then you're mad,

Then you're screaming out, "why me?" -

But you finally see that's how it's got to be:

You were born and bred to run

When you hear the starting gun,

Never looking back, eyes fixed on the track -

'Til you can't keep up the pace.

No one ever wins the race,

But the time has given you a human face.

Don't complain you had no choice -

Until now, you had no voice

And if you knew how hard it was you'd say, "I can't,"

Susanna Dark

And it's the only way I know

For a baby soul to grow:

You've got to hoe the row before you plant.


If you need me in the night,

I am there before you call.


If you stumble, I am there before you fall.

If you trust in only me,

I will give you light to see

And the proof is in the truth that sets you free:

'Cause you should be full of joy,

Not an angry drunkard's toy

Or a narrow-minded preacher's whipping boy.

Susanna Dark

## How to use The Celtic Cross Spread

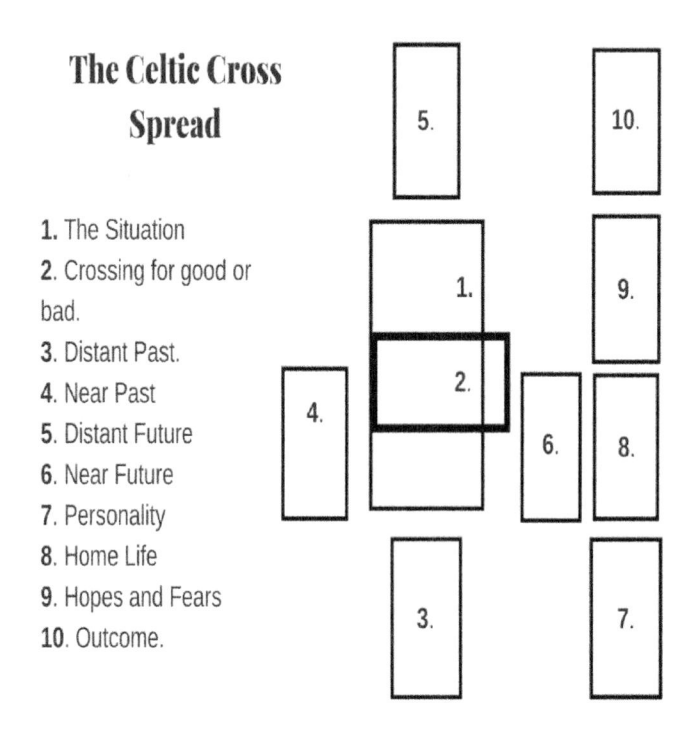

**The Celtic Cross Spread**

1. The Situation
2. Crossing for good or bad.
3. Distant Past.
4. Near Past
5. Distant Future
6. Near Future
7. Personality
8. Home Life
9. Hopes and Fears
10. Outcome.

- Start by shuffling the cards and whilst you shuffle still your mind of any other thoughts, apart from the question that you wish to ask the cards itself.

- When you can sense that you are ready, proceed by laying face up card number one in the centre of the spread. This card is the current situation.

- Follow by card number two, now this card is what is crossing the current situation for good or bad. Meaning for example, if the situation is a relationship issue and card one,showed the king of cups and card two is the queen of swords, it could represent that the man we are looking at in the reading has another woman in his life, for better or worse. The words "Crossing the current situation for good or bad" means this is a help or a hindrance.

- Card three is the distant past and look at what could be affecting or causing the current situation. Could this be a distant memory that is creating a current unrealistic perspective on the situation.

- Same for card four, but this is the near past. So, this is the immediate events or event that has happened to affect the current situation.

- Card number five, is the near future, what is coming up imminently.

- Card number six is the card for the distant future.

- Card number seven is the client's personality. How are they feeling at present? What type of personality do they have? How is this situation affecting them?

- Card number eight is the client's home life. Are they happy in their home, and what are they carrying with them emotionally with regards to other areas of their life?

- Card number nine is the hopes and fears card. What is the clients hopes and fears over the situation itself.

- Card number ten is the final card and the outcome card.

- Remember though that when conducting a reading using this spread you can link cards together. If you are looking at a card and thinking, I am getting nothing out of the card, look to the left or right of the card and see if the cards link together and see if they can help you with the information you are needing. Remember the whole spread is there to help you so use it wisely. Nothing is set in stone. You can read it how you want to, you are, remember, reading the cards intuitively.

**The Hanged Man** – See Things Differently

## Image - Fortitude (Strength)

### The card of Inner Strength

Susanna Dark

## Image - Death

## The Card of Death and Rebirth

Susanna Dark

## References

**Alchemy and the grail, Tareth.**
http://www.beliefnet.com/columnists/intentchopra/2010/06/the-mystery-of-illness.html"illness.
https://www.thejourney.com/blog/the-real-cause-of-your-disease/
https://www.nhs.uk/conditions/obesity/causes/
http://obesity.ygoy.com/emotional-causes-of-obesity/
https://www.thoughtco.com/god-goddess-healing-ritual-2562842
https://www.aetherius.org/healing-yourself-and-others/
https://www.nhs.uk/conditions/generalised-anxiety-disorder/
https://en.wikipedia.org/wiki/Self-healing
https://www.essentiallifeskills.net/develop-your-intuition.html
https://hellopoetry.com/words/tarot/

**All tarot card images purchased from Shutterstock.com**

Susanna Dark

Printed in Great Britain
by Amazon